CPSIA information can be obtained
at www.ICGtesting.com
Printed in the USA
JSHW032352270821
18267JS00002B/112

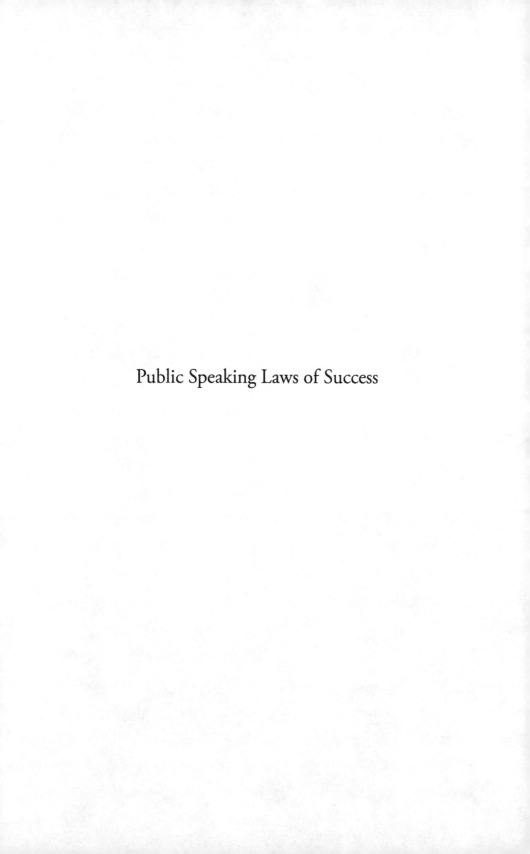

Public Speaking Laws of Success

ENDORSEMENTS

"Reading this book has made me realize what an honor it has been for me to participate in several ELO events and I wish to heartily recommend it to all who aspire to public speaking, no matter how competent they think they are. It makes for compulsive reading, being a delightful distillation of years of experience that is full of (sometimes hilarious) illustrative stories of what can go right, and, more importantly, what can go wrong with attempts to communicate to an audience. Its practical wisdom rings true to experience to such an extent that if I had read it fifty years ago, it would have saved me having to learn many things the hard way. Reading it now may well save me from many more!"

John C. Lennox, Professor Emeritus of Mathematics & Associate Fellow, Saïd Business School, University of Oxford

"This book captures, in 50 laws based on stories, all the things you need to know about the basics of public speaking to be part of the top 10% of all speakers you ever hear. The risk of not reading this book and still speaking in public will be costly—don't be collateral damage on the road to your dreams."

Pat Williams, NBA Hall of Famer & author of *R evolutionary Leadership*, Orlando, FL

"This book could not come at a better time, when many of us are required to do some form of public speaking such as in a Zoom session, which can be very daunting in an open session or in making presentations and pitches. The principles that Rick Goossen outlines in his book are highly practical, useful, 'easy to use and grasp' with a broad appeal reflecting Rick's lifelong passion for speaking well whether in public or private. From an Asian viewpoint, where public speaking or speaking in class is often not natural, this is a very instructive book for those who are grappling with this required skill for the new economy. The first book I read about public speaking was by Dale Carnegie; I wish I would have been able to first read this book."

Dr Bill Foo, Chair, Tung Lok Group & Advisory Board, Salvation Army, Singapore

"I wish Rick Goossen's valuable book *Public Speaking Laws of Success* had been published years ago as it would have improved my speaking abilities a lot. *Public Speaking Laws of Success* will enable you to become a more competent and confident speaker. I highly recommend you buy this book and read its stimulating stories and learn some of the inside habits and secrets of successful speakers. I am sure you will enjoy this book and find it a valuable resource in developing your speaking skills."

Dr. Peter Legge, OBC, LLD (HON), CPAE, CSP, HOF, Chair and CEO of Canada Wide Media Ltd., Vancouver, Canada

"Listening to a poor speaker is bad: hiring one is worse. Rick hires speakers, so he knows from a lifetime's mixture of scintillation and squirming what works and what doesn't. He has distilled fifty principles from this experience, which can turn a novice into a veteran and a seasoned speaker into a sought-after expert. This easy-to-read book will help you become an easy-to-listen-to speaker, and I recommend it to all who have a modicum of compassion towards long-suffering audiences!"

Rev. Dr Michael Lloyd, Principal, Wycliffe Hall, University of Oxford

"Rick Goossen has done it again! *Public Speaking Laws of Success* offers readers a timely, practical and real-world handbook for all manner of speaking engagements. Reading it, and using it as a tool, will dramatically raise your effectiveness as a public speaker and, perhaps even more importantly, your overall power of persuasion as a communicator. He is that rare force in the world of public speaking who organizes important speaking events, is an avid audience member who listens to great speakers around the world, and is a world-class public speaker himself. In short, he has achieved the 'trifecta' of public speaking! After presenting and teaching our research on entrepreneurship to over six million people, in some forty countries, across nine languages, and for the past four decades, we have learned a few things about public speaking. And one thing I know for sure—*Public Speaking Laws of Success* is a book I wish I had read forty years ago!"

Larry C. Farrell, Founder/Chair, the Farrell Company, VA & AZ

"Whether you're making the business presentation your career hangs on, or you've been asked to emcee the upcoming holiday party, this new book from my friend Rick Goossen will equip you for success. This is not only an essential, great read for any budding or experienced public speaker, it's entertaining while revealing its many insights. And these public speaking truth nuggets travel well, just like the author. Whether you're speaking in the north, south, east, or west, each law is grounded in Rick's unique experience—and he's had lots of it. Like every event Rick designs or speaks at, this book will keep you entertained with real-to-life stories, illustrations, and examples that clearly make and powerfully reinforce the main point. Don't speak in public without it!"

Dr. Gary Lindblad, Dean, Crowell School of Business,
Biola University, La Mirada, CA, USA

"Rick Goossen is an expert at obtaining maximum impact. Whether discussing financial investments, organizing a conference, or delivering a speech, he instinctively knows how to get enviable results. Now you have access to his considerable wisdom. Communication has never been more critical. In this insightful, practical, highly readable book, he will help you become a speaker who moves people to action."

Richard Blackaby, President, Blackaby Ministries International,
author of *Experiencing God* and *Spiritual Leadership,* Jonesboro, GA

"Rick is not just an excellent public speaker personally. He has also studied many masters of this craft up close and personal. I'm confident this book will be chock-full of valuable wisdom for those looking to hone their craft of communicating from the stage."

Jordan Raynor, national bestselling author of
Called to Create and Master of One, Tampa, FL

"Over the past three decades or so, I have been an emcee and spoken at many webinars and conferences on all the major continents around the world. I have never, ever read a book that's as relevant and practical as Dr. Rick Goossen's *Public Speaking Laws of Success*. Having roots in Vancouver, and now living in Hong Kong, I can attest that Rick's book will appeal to a wide array of readers in both the West and the East, as all of us can get so much out of this 'true bible of public speaking!'"

Eric C.L. Poon, FCIM, Executive Vice Chair, Association of Family Offices in Asia, and Founder, ePGA, Hong Kong SAR, CHINA

"As a fellow speaker, and even more so, as an audience member, I implore you to read this book and help raise your personal speaking game. I've done a lot of speaking at public events, which means I've also had to sit through a lot of speaking at public events. I've heard some of the best and some of the worst. Mostly, I've heard mediocrity. That's tragic, because as Rick Goossen shows, mediocrity is optional. It's not that speakers decide to be bland and meandering, it's that they don't decide not to be."

Jerry Bowyer, entrepreneur, economist, author & public speaker, Pittsburgh, PA

"Everyone who strives for growth and stepping up as a leader will need to master the skills of public speaking. I have known Rick for many years. He is not just an exceptional speaker, but also a man who always delivers and makes an impact. *Public Speaking Laws of Success* is truly a must-read for any leader or leader-to-be."

Justin Leung, Board Member, YCP Holdings Limited, Advisor for Hong Kong Cyberport, an entrepreneur and devoted educator, Hong Kong SAR, CHINA

"Success in public speaking leaves clues. Rick Goossen has not only mastered public speaking for himself, but has interviewed, studied, and spent time with some of the greatest speakers alive today. I am calling this the must-read book for achieving mastery in public speaking. This book will be your guidebook for unleashing your potential to become a great public speaker."

Brad Pedersen, Co-founder & Chair of Open Mind Developments Corporation (Pela), Kelowna, BC & Hong Kong SAR

PUBLIC SPEAKING

FOR EVERYONE AND EVERY OCCASION

LAWS OF SUCCESS

RICHARD J. GOOSSEN

NEW YORK

LONDON • NASHVILLE • MELBOURNE • VANCOUVER

PUBLIC SPEAKING LAWS OF SUCCESS

For Everyone and Every Occasion

Published in New York, New York, by Morgan James Publishing. Morgan James is a trademark of Morgan James, LLC. www.MorganJamesPublishing.com

ISBN 9781631954542 paperback
ISBN 9781631954559 eBook
Library of Congress Control Number: 2020951176

Cover and Interior Design by:
Chris Treccani
www.3dogcreative.net

Morgan James is a proud partner of Habitat for Humanity Peninsula and Greater Williamsburg. Partners in building since 2006.

Get involved today! Visit
MorganJamesPublishing.com/giving-back

FOR THE REST OF THE G10:

Brenda
Brooke
Rob
Matthias
Kia
Jacoba
Neil
Amanda
Kaylyn

TABLE OF CONTENTS

ACKNOWLEDGMENTS

I would like to thank everyone who helped make this book possible. I am grateful to the many excellent speakers that have worked with me over the years. I refer to many individuals throughout the book who have enriched both my life and many events I have organized, taught me lessons in public speaking, and have also demonstrated great character and graciousness on and off the platform.

One particular speaker deserves a special mention. Peter Legge, my friend and the writer of this book's foreword, has spoken at a number of events I have organized and he has always done an outstanding job. He is justifiably ranked among the top twenty public speakers in North America. I have learned much by simply spending time with him, both at events and over meals.

Most importantly, of course, my family has been a great support. I would like to thank my longsuffering spouse who has given me the space to indulge in my time-consuming joy of writing at the expense of other commitments. She has endured thirty-four years, thus far, of my public speaking to an audience of one. My wife has enjoyed each one of my books that she has read. My kids have been subjected to decades of my lecturing, and my kids-in-law have been availed of the same opportunity more recently.

My kids have experienced my joy of speaking, whether to an audience of one or many. For example, at the age of around seven or eight, one of my sons did something he shouldn't have. As I was explaining, apparently at some length, the inadvisability of that particular course of action, he shouted to my wife upstairs, "Dad won't stop talking to me!" Truly a fate worse than corporal punishment.

I have appreciated working with the team at Morgan James Publishing. They have been very professional and helpful at every step of the way, and a pleasure to work with.

I would like to thank Logan Ferguson, who did an excellent job of assisting with editing and proofreading the manuscript of this book.

I need to thank all the people and organizations that have given me an opportunity to hone my own craft of public speaking over the years. Public speakers need an audience and the biggest challenge can be to have a chance to work on your skills. I am grateful for the early opportunities, many of which came in a church context (not quite like a young Whitney Houston singing in her church choir, but similar idea). I wish I could go back and thank every one of the parishioners for their patience.

Ultimately, *Public Speaking Laws of Success* is based on what I have learned from others. I have simply organized and recorded the laws and told the stories behind them.

FOREWORD

Let me take you back over sixty years to when my parents and I had first immigrated to Greater Vancouver, Canada. That year, upon graduating from junior high, the school asked me to speak and address the graduating students. I was a bit nervous, but nevertheless, I jumped at the opportunity and enjoyed the experience.

After that speech, I was hooked on the prospect of being a professional speaker. After I entered high school, I often found myself giving a speech in most of the assemblies or as emcee of an event.

When I finished high school, I began to speak all over Vancouver for free. This allowed my skills to develop. I joined the National Speaker's Association in the United States as well as the Canadian equivalent, the Canadian Association of Professional Speakers. Over the years, it has been my honor to have spoken to over five thousand audiences on over five continents, and every province in Canada.

As I developed as a speaker, I received many accolades along the way, including the privilege of receiving the Toastmasters International Golden Gavel Award. Many well-known celebrities have also received this award, such as Earl Nightingale, Dr. Nido Qubein, Tony Robbins, Zig Ziglar, John Maxwell, and Walter Cronkite, which puts me in excellent company. I have been fortunate enough to have been invited to speak at many conventions around the world, perhaps the most important of which was to join the Speakers Roundtable, which consists of the top 20 speakers and influencers in North America. I am the only Canadian that has been invited to join.

The privilege of the platform and public speaking is not as easy as it looks or as you might think. Yes, I have been successful in this area, but

I wish Rick Goossen's valuable book, *Public Speaking Laws of Success,* had been published years ago. It would have improved my speaking abilities a lot faster, because it is packed with stories and advice to help you be more than just a run of the mill speaker. At some point, you will be asked to emcee a wedding, address a Board of Directors, or speak at various large companies, Christmas parties, or AGMs which might eventually lead to other speaking engagements. Rick's new book is jammed with clear examples to help you learn the intricacies of the business and avoid its many pitfalls. *Public Speaking Laws of Success* will enable you to become a more competent and confident speaker. I highly recommend everyone buy this book, read its stimulating stories, and learn some of the habits and secrets of successful speakers. I am sure readers will enjoy this book and find it a valuable resource in developing their speaking skills.

Dr. Peter Legge, OBC, LLD (HON), CPAE, CSP, HOF
Chair and CEO of Canada Wide Media Ltd

INTRODUCTION

Have you ever spoken in public? If so, do you want to improve? In just two hours, this book will teach you the 50 public speaking laws of success so that you can be better than 90% of all the public speakers you'll ever hear.

Why write a book about public speaking? Like everyone, I have been part of more cringe-inducing presentations than I can count. I have seen weddings thrown off the rails and families embarrassed. I have seen banquets completely derailed due to a self-serving speaker. I have seen the life and oxygen sucked out of a room due to an inappropriate remark from the podium. I have seen memorial services where the dearly departed have not done so in dignity. I have listened to speakers that wasted everyone's time and made both themselves and the organizers look like buffoons. I have seen business presentations that backfired so badly that the speaker and company would have been better off not appearing at all. The most aggravating part is that all these mistakes can be prevented. All anyone needs to speak well is a bit of preparation and an understanding of the public speaking laws of success. My passion is to help people be more successful in their public speaking, to help them help themselves, to make the world safe from such cringe-inducing sessions, and, yes, to achieve world peace.

Few public speakers, including the great ones, have received any formal training in public speaking. Those who have still usually have only minimal training, certainly nothing significant compared to the success they have achieved. That's great news! One of the unique aspects of public speaking is that, while it is a distinct skill set, there is generally no barrier to entry and self-improvement. Of course, this is a two-sided coin. People get opportunities to speak unrelated to their ability to do so. It is their expertise or reputation in a particular field that opens doors for them.

In your own case, people may just want to hear you share what you know—regardless of how well you say it. As a result, you need to recognize that, whatever your expertise in a particular area, being a good public speaker is an entirely separate skill set. One does not transfer to another, at least not entirely. Half of success is what you know, and the other half is how you say it. Remember, no one may care if Warren Buffett is an effective public speaker, but if Buffett were an unknown economic analyst from Nebraska, public speaking skills would be essential in getting his ideas heard.

There are too many speakers who assume that because of their expertise, they will be able to speak about their specialty effectively in public. This is demonstrated regularly not to be the case. Perhaps there is an assumption that they will "learn it as they go." This will only happen by design. Only a very small minority of speakers can simply figure it out as they go along. Plan on the fact that you likely aren't one of them, and commit yourself to learning the art of public speaking.

All of the public speaking laws of success that I discuss in this book are based on decades of practical experience. My experience is described in the "About the Author" section at the end of this book. I would like to highlight one particular source of experience that I refer to throughout the book, which is Entrepreneurial Leaders Organization, or "ELO"(www. ELONetwork.org). The origins of ELO go back to 2005. Since that time I have organized over 60 events ("ELO Forums") and programs around the world. Through ELO I have worked with many top speakers, emceed many events, and learned a lot about all aspects of public speaking. The stories I recount in this book are rooted in events that happened, people I knew, and situations in which I found myself. Wherever it is a positive example, I refer to the speaker by name, so you will see references to people like John Maxwell, Mark Burnett, Pat Williams and Peter Legge, to name a few. At the other end of the spectrum are people more notable for breaching the laws of public speaking, rather than observing them. In order to spare any embarrassment (after all, we all have bad days), I don't refer to those individuals by name, or I change a few details about the event so people can't be identified. Either way, the key point is that the situations actually happened and are examples to learn from. The goal is for this book to be an original work, as reflected in the Table of Contents, and not based on summarizing other people's research on the topic.

The book itself is structured around fifty public speaking laws of success. The laws are interrelated and complementary. In some cases where there is particularly strong synergy, I point out a reference in one chapter specifically to a law in another chapter.

The first section covers what I call "the mechanics." These are the most basic skills of public speaking. You may have seen some of these basics covered elsewhere, but likely not all of them, or in the manner in which I present them. For example, in Chapter 21, I talk about "the most dangerous 15 seconds of any presentation."

The second section highlights the "key principles" to bear in mind when speaking in public so you can avoid common pitfalls. The principles and examples selected are, again, all based on experience. This section is intended to provide some more advanced concepts beyond the foundational mechanics of the first section.

The third section deals with the "digital environment." More and more, public speaking and presentations are conducted in an online environment, and video conferences services are an increasingly preferred means of communication. How does a public speaker adapt to that context? Many classic laws of public presenting still apply—but there are several unique aspects to bear in mind in the digital landscape, as well.

The fourth section focuses on the "applications." If you pick up this book because you are about to emcee a wedding or speak at a funeral, then you can turn to the chapter dedicated specifically to those events for some specific pointers. I cover most applications in this section. However, while there are different contexts, the basic public speaking laws of success from the previous sections still apply.

As the subtitle of this book indicates, these laws are for everyone and for every occasion. While this book will certainly help you prepare for a TED Talk (a real one, not just a TEDx talk—we'll talk more about the difference in Law #25), that is not the main intent. The purpose of *Public Speaking Laws of Success* is to help you competently perform public speaking in personal and business contexts. This book is not intended for one-off "set pieces," like performing a monologue in a play, that require and demand an extreme amount of preparation. My objective is not to cover the minutiae of very specific forms of presentation, but rather address the core laws which are the foundation for all forms of public speaking in many contexts.

If you're one of those readers who's been given the opportunity to do a TED Talk, that's great! Most people, though, are not here to prepare for anything quite so extensive. Instead, you need to know how to competently emcee your nephew's upcoming wedding, or prepare a fitting tribute for a memorial service. Likewise, if you are doing a business presentation, no matter how important, you cannot justify taking the time to prepare endlessly or excessively for a presentation: you have another one coming up the week after. You don't have the time, nor often the interest or the advance notice necessary to prepare for months on end. What you need is the basics to do a great job.

Lastly, most books on public speaking will highlight the opportunities that arise for those who can speak well in public. So it should be. Public speaking is a distinct skill that is honed and developed through practice. Those who speak well in public get various benefits. First, you are positioned as an expert, giving you the opportunity to demonstrate your knowledge. You are able to build your personal brand, and depending upon your business, you may have a greater opportunity to promote your product and/or service. Second, you may have a perspective or opinion on a certain issue, and being a good public speaker builds up a platform that gives you the ability to share your views. Lastly, by demonstrating competence, you may get some unexpected career opportunities. You never know who is in the audience. Over the years, I have received numerous teaching and speaking assignments and, yes, job opportunities, because of the people who were in the audience.

A final caveat, however. Public speaking is like compound interest: it can work for you or against you. If you do well in public speaking, the positive results will accumulate like compounding interest on an investment, building exponentially. If, by contrast, you do a poor job, the compounding works in reverse. Your reputation suffers and you are building momentum in the wrong direction, like piling up debt. The interest keeps accumulating against you.

If you follow the laws of this book, though, you *will* have compounding success.

Read on.

A—THE MECHANICS

A.1: WHAT, ME WORRY?

"What, me worry?" Alfred E. Neuman, the fictional character of the satirical *Mad Magazine*, provided inspiration for public speakers everywhere. The 50 public speaking laws of success in this book are intended to give you the confidence to know you will be in the top 10% of all public speakers, so you don't need to worry at all.

Yes, many people are nervous at the thought of public speaking. It's often said that most people fear public speaking more than they fear death, so, as Jerry Seinfeld once pointed out, plenty of people doing a eulogy might prefer to be the ones in the coffin.

As I have taught public speaking skills to over a thousand students over the years, I saw some quite tragic circumstances. One sticks out in particular. In an upper year class, I had groups of students do a major presentation for a significant chunk of their final grade. Each student was responsible for a 20-minute presentation.

I could see as this student made his way to the front of the classroom that he seemed to be a bit stiff and uptight. Was it because of his newly-purchased, too tight suit? He then began his presentation in a halting, staccato-like fashion. Within minutes, he seemed to be hyperventilating. I was a bit startled, though of course I didn't show it, as I had never had this happen before. He barely hung on to complete his presentation, which he cut mercifully short. Clearly, nerves had gotten the better of him.

So, how is one to combat fears around public speaking? Let's discard a few shibboleths at the outset.

"Just go up there and be yourself." No, don't. That's a bad idea. Yes, be authentic, but prepare to present a polished, professional version of yourself—otherwise, you might look like an ill-prepared rube that just fell off the back of a turnip truck.

Another popular mistake is to "imagine the audience is naked." Everyone's heard that suggestion, but I don't advise following it. I guess the theory is that it boosts your confidence, but I'm not sure that's a mental picture anyone wants in their head. Put it in the dustbin of public speaking history.

A similar pacifier is the saying that "you are not performing." That's not true; if you want to be more than a person speaking, who happens to be doing it in front of others, you need to think of it like a performance. This means that you need to have a sense of your role, your audience, and the best way to communicate with them. Yes, being onstage will have an impact on how you speak—let it empower and embolden, not eviscerate, you.

Worry is fought through a combination of preparation and experience. Like anything in life, if you are prepared in advance, there is a limit to how far off the rails you can go, and you can have a few backup plans in place to get you back on track if things do go sideways.

Don't put undue pressure on yourself regarding the details. Instead, focus on the big picture message that you are trying to communicate. You may know your presentation largely from memory, but it's still helpful to refer to your presentation slides or notes, as necessary. For example, don't say, "I want to explain five points," and then try to do so from memory alone. Either write out the points on your presentation screen, or, if you are going from memory, say, "Here are some important points on this topic" (that way, if you forget one, people won't know how many points you were going to cover).

It is also fine to acknowledge to yourself that you might be nervous. Think of nerves as energy that can be positively channeled. It puts all your senses on full alert; you are ready to respond to anything. This energy should not be allowed to disrupt your concentration, but instead should be channeled to get you fired up for a great presentation.

You also have to put yourself in the mindset that any public speaking opportunity is a chance to deliver a message to positively impact people. You should be excited about it, raring and ready to go like the hounds about to be released. When I am about to speak somewhere, I always feel like I want to run out on stage. I am excited to get going. I look forward to sharing something I think is of value. I get amped up. Once the positive energy is harnessed, it also pushes out negativity.

Of course, there is a difference between knowing how to deal with fears around public speaking and then mastering those fears when actually doing the public speaking. This is easier said than done. An important core principle is to practice as much as possible, which will allow you to become increasingly comfortable on the platform. You will do an increasing number of things effortlessly (i.e., voice intonation, avoidance of filler words, head movement, controlled hand movement, proper pace and use of silence, etc.) You no longer need to fret about the core mechanics of public speaking as they have been incorporated into your speaking style. Like mastering a golf swing.

Of course, your ability to handle nervous energy and channel it positively will be a reflection as to how you handle things generally. This book cannot, of course, address deep-seated issues with anxiety or self-esteem. We can, however, provide laws for you to use after learning elsewhere how best to channel your inner Alfred E. Neuman.

Stefanie Hartman, a professional speaker and marketing guru, has some advice on successfully calming presentation jitters: "What helped me calm my nerves was to have my speech be focused on the people attending." In a conversation I had with her, she elaborated on this idea. "When I walk on stage, my role is of a guide to their success. I am there for them every step of the way, laughing, listening, and helping, and not making it about me." Stefanie said this method allows her never to feel self-conscious on stage. "My focus is not me," she explained, "it's about the person and people seeking my help."

LAW #1: Any nervousness should be channeled into positive energy that will help you be fully alert and ready to seize the opportunity to positively impact an audience.

A.2: ATTENTION, PLEASE!

The boisterous throng had been in a holding pattern for almost an hour, guests mingling in the reception prior to the formal banquet and circling the bar like sharks in a feeding frenzy. They now bumbled their way into the ballroom, plunked unevenly onto chairs around their banquet tables with yet more bottles of red and white pleading to be opened. This evening's speaker had the formidable task of attempting to impose some semblance of order to this chaos, like shining a light into darkness.

With great trepidation, one Father O'Brien made his way to the podium, clearly having drawn the short straw among the organizers. To kick things off, Father O'Brien came to the podium to offer a preliminary prayer, skipping an introduction. The good Father, an earnest young priest fresh from the Emerald Isle, leaned into the microphone and, perhaps thinking that the holiness of the moment would trump the crowd's red-faced glee, said in his thick Irish accent: "In the Name of the Father!" The buzz continued unabated. He tried again, like a farmer throwing his seeds on rocky soil. Then he bellowed into the microphone: *"In the name of the Father!"* That got everyone's attention—and presumably God's, too. It was a bit undignified, but it worked. He was able to proceed with his prayer.

This event was an annual fundraiser for a private Catholic boys' school held at a swank downtown hotel. Father O'Brien's strategy, however, was one of many options. I have witnessed many ways that speakers have tried to get people's attention, from the subtle to the overt, and some ways are much more effective (and professional) than others. You may be used to speaking at larger venues and at well-organized events, but if you are speaking at random places and at irregular times—such as emceeing or doing talks to small crowds—then your first job may be to get everyone's

5

attention! Before we even get to the mechanics of public speaking, you need to know how to get started in a situation like this one.

You may be asked to the podium while the crowd is still merrily chatting away. Everyone is there to meet and greet each other, and the excuse is your presentation as a public speaker. You are welcomed to the podium, but barely anyone beyond the first few rows notices. Then the inexperienced organizer leaves you at the podium, hoping that things will sort themselves out.

So your job as a public speaker is to get everyone's attention. This is not always easy. I have heard some people advise simply standing there and waiting. And waiting. The idea is that eventually the crowd will quieten on its own. I may run with unique crowds, but in my experience, that can be quite time-consuming.

You don't want to waste too much time waiting, and you do want to maintain your poise and not start barking out orders—but what do you do? After having organized many events and having gained a rudimentary understanding of human psychology, I humbly suggest the following.

The ELO Forums I run typically have around 300 people. Before a speaker begins, the attendees are almost always chatting with each other, and there is a palpable sense of energy in the room. Simply going up to the podium and asking for attention rarely works. Somewhat comically, if a speaker then tries to speak louder, everyone else simply speaks louder to be heard, too!

One alternative to the O'Brien method is to provide an alternative clue. You can quickly flicker the lights, or turn them off and on with long pauses. This works to some extent, but not perfectly. Our attendees have often demonstrated that they can speak in the dark. Another approach is to stimulate one of the other senses: make an alternative or unusual sound. A number of hotels will have a bell or a xylophone for a person to use from the podium, or to send someone else scurrying throughout the crowd with it. That actually works, getting people's attention much more quickly.

Another valuable way to manage people's attention is to work with the audio visual team. They can control the sound and the lights simultaneously, thereby escalating the solution to a two-pronged attack. Sometimes playing music works to get everyone's attention. Again, though, that can cause people to simply start speaking more loudly. Another alternative is to start a video, which then precedes the speaker to the podium. This is a good way to get people's attention. Once the lights go out, the video starts with the sound cranked up, and as people settle down the volume is reduced.

Another way of getting the attention of an audience, which I don't recommend but which I offer as a contrarian reference point, is the opposite. During my first year at McGill Law School, we had a legendary professor named Paul-André Crépeau. He deserved much respect, none of which was afforded him by his first year law students. The class was held in a small, tiered, U-shaped auditorium that was sized for about 150 students. The class was about half that number, with students spread throughout the room. Like most students, people would chat after coming in, not too concerned about when the class would start.

At the appointed start of the class, Prof. Crépeau wouldn't try to get everyone's attention. He wouldn't raise his voice. He would simply, very quietly, start teaching. Only the first few rows could hear him. After five to ten minutes other students would realize that the class had started and that something being said might end up on an exam. Then students would start to quiet down and whisper to other students to do the same. As the class gradually quieted, Prof. Crépeau would slowly raise his voice. It worked well, and it was low-stress for him.

There are simpler situations when you start speaking to a group, as well. I am the Director of the Entrepreneurial Leaders Programme, which is held each summer in collaboration with Wycliffe Hall, University of Oxford. We have about 25 business leaders from around the world. Before the session begins, there is a lot of chatter, but when you take to the podium they are generally ready to begin. This is a fine balance of encouraging, cajoling, directing people to the podium. People are there to build relationships, in addition to learning. So, it's not simply a matter of herding cats to start on time, but allowing people to fulfill one of the purposes for which they came to the course.

When possible, as a speaker, you should try to ensure that the crowd is quiet before you go to the podium. You want to go up and start right away with your presentation. It can look somewhat undignified if you are the one having to get everyone's attention. I have been in that situation too many times, looking frazzled—although providing comedic relief to the first few rows—while trying to quell the unruly mob.

The bottom line is that there is generally no point in beginning your presentation unless people are listening. Try not to be in the position where you need to get everyone's attention. You want to be able to get to the podium and start your talk.

LAW #2: Ideally, the audience is settled before you come to the podium and you can start your presentation, but be prepared to settle the crowd yourself. Don't start speaking unless you are being heard.

A.3: THE ONE-MINUTE TEST

The speaker had just finished his keynote. Right afterwards, he came down from the platform and bumped into one of the listeners, heading for the exit. The listener politely said, "Good presentation. Thanks for coming."

The speaker pressed for more. "What did you like best?"

The listener responded: "The ending." With that, he was gone.

Don't let that be you.

How can you assess a presentation, whether you are the speaker or the listener? Try doing this test sometime: exactly one minute after a person has finished speaking, ask yourself what you can recall. Do you remember the title? Do you remember any of the points?

You likely remember some of the stories told, if they were good ones (see Law #5). We all learn through stories, and they tend to stick in our memory. A good story may make for great public speaking, but is it teaching? Can you remember the point of the story, or do you only remember the story's outline, with no idea how it tied into the key points of the presentation?

What else do you remember? Maybe there were some good jokes or one-liners that got a laugh from the crowd. You may have thought, hey, that's a good one, and it stuck in your mind.

A bad presentation is like Pablum for the mind: it tastes great, but it isn't filling. You listened to someone for, say, 30 minutes, and it was entertaining, but you can't remember a thing.

That's fine for a comedy show, but not if it is a business presentation, board meeting, or any other venue where it is important to get a message across. I have heard experienced speakers tell a joke, get a muffled laugh, and then say, "It has nothing to do with my talk, but I thought it was funny." That's disrespectful, arrogant, and distracting.

Public speaking is communicating. A good communicator is able to make things stick. Are there some presentations that you can remember months, and even years, later? Why? What makes them memorable?

On August 28, 1963 at the March on Washington for Jobs and Freedom, Rev. Martin Luther King Jr. delivered his now-famous "I have a dream" speech to an estimated 250,000 people. He used the phrase "I have a dream" nine times. Towards the end of his speech he used the phrase "let freedom ring" nine times. Why this repetition? To clearly get his message across. Clarity is enhanced through careful and skillful repetition. This is very different from the written form, where repetition is generally not encouraged. Remember, public speaking is not public reading.

To determine if you are a great communicator, next time you do a presentation, ask a handful of people immediately afterwards what the presentation was about. What was the thrust or thesis, and what were the supporting points? You may be surprised or depressed to find that immediately after your presentation, people can't remember virtually anything about it. This is why speaking is an art form all its own. You need to learn how to emphasize key points, keep them well-organized, and make your words easy to remember.

This "one-minute test" reinforces so many of this book's public speaking laws of success. What was the point of the presentation? What was the structure? How were the points organized? Were they easy to remember? Did the speaker keep reinforcing the overall point, transition well from one point to another, and then pull all the points together?

The old adage makes sense: say what you're going to say; say it; and then say what you just said!

LAW #3: Use the "one-minute test" to assess whether you have delivered or heard a great presentation.

A.4: THE HOOK

Ask yourself candidly: why should anyone listen to you? People make a quick decision, typically within seconds and definitely in one minute or less, about whether they should tune in or tune out. They are making a judgment as you are introduced and walking to the podium. Bear that in mind. You have less than a minute to get their attention. How are you going to do that?

You need a hook.

As with written and online forms of communication, you need something to get people's attention. There are different ways to do this. You can start off with a provocative question, a gripping story or a unique fact, or an observation.

Let me give an example of provocative questions from one of my standard presentations to the non-profit sector. I have worked with various non-profit organizations on how to source and build relationships with high net worth donors. I start off my presentation with two simple and provocative questions. First: "Why would anyone want to give to your organization?" This is a bit of an opening jolt. Perhaps they have never heard it put so bluntly, but that is the question that potential donors are asking. The responses may not be well thought out. "Well, because… uh, we're doing good stuff. And, uh, we've got a track record. And, you know, uh, we help people in need." None of those answers are good enough, and the response indicates a lack of deep thought on the issue. Lots of non-profits do good work. There must be a unique value proposition.

I then follow up with a second question: "Is what you are offering to donors matched by why donors are supporting you?" I ask this second question to be thought-provoking. I ask because often non-profit organizations are not actually clear on why people support them. They don't have a clear idea as to the profile of their donors. A particularly interesting dynamic of the non-profit sector is that the people paying or supporting an organization are not the people receiving the service (i.e., donors supporting a homeless shelter typically aren't using the shelter themselves). This is different from the basic commercial transaction for most of us: I pay for a service (i.e. at a restaurant) and I receive the services (i.e. I eat the food). I know the quality of what I am paying for by receiving the product. Donors don't usually have (or want) that opportunity.

Non-profit organizations need to think carefully about what they do uniquely well. Why should I make giving to your charity—above thousands of others—my priority? Now that they're thinking it through in their own minds, I can follow up with, "In this presentation I'll address how I can help your non-profit make a compelling case as to why high net worth donors should make your organization a priority."

I have done this presentation countless times. It is engaging from the outset. I can see the wheels turning inside people's heads. Once they are engaged and have tried to answer for themselves, we can go through the presentation. I find this opening hook to be straightforward and effective—and it is tied into the presentation.

A second potential hook is to start a presentation with a unique fact. Try, however, to make it unique to you, your expertise and your research. You and everyone else have heard about the Internet and know how to search on Google. "Did you know how many bees there are in the world?" is not the best starter. Your audience may not know how many bees there are, but it's easy enough to look up. Instead, do something more unique. I find that proprietary research can often be compelling. I once had a speaker from a think tank who had done research on attitudes toward faith in society. His presentation was chock-full of interesting statistics. He pointed out that 90% of people pray. He then pointed out the humorous conclusion that 80% of people believe in God. So, clearly, more people pray to God than believe He exists.

In my own case, I have a source of unique information. I have interviewed approximately 500 Christian entrepreneurs around the world over the past 15 years. The result has been five edited books, one book, research reports, hundreds of blogs and about 100 e-interviews published. This is the largest study of its kind, as far as I am aware. I have a structured interview format where I ask a variety of questions related to faith and work. One of the questions I ask: "What has been your lowest moment?" It's an intentionally broad question to see how people will respond. When I am doing a presentation I ask the audience, what do you think the most common response was? After a pause to let the audience ponder the question, I then share the results of my research. I disclose that despite such a broad question, one answer commonly comes up. The answer is not something people commonly talk about, but rather something to move on from. I have had people break down in tears when giving this response to my question.

What is this response? "I was betrayed." A friend put money ahead of a relationship, and the response is not, "I lost money," or "I lost a friend." Rather, the most common answer is betrayal: "I put my trust in someone. I relied on them and took them into my confidence, and they breached that trust." Think of the legal concept of a trust document. It's like a fiduciary duty was violated. You relied on a person, and that person let you down. People have had their companies and relationships permanently undermined.

I describe some examples to the audience, and then ask, "Have you ever been betrayed? Have you put your trust in someone and then been let down?" The above discussion of the research and the focus on betrayal gets people's attention.

A third form of hook is to open your presentation with a story. In the following law (#5) I describe one particular story in more detail, but in this law I will simply provide an overview. Stories about well-known figures often garner interest. Whether you're talking about Winston Churchill or William Shakespeare, coming up with some interesting facts will get people's attention.

You can retell a friend's stories, or those of famous people, but especially when you are starting off, tell your own. The more you tell it, the more skilled you will be at helping people see themselves in the story.

People learn from stories and they remember stories, but storytelling is an art form. I have had many people who can't tell their own story well. You need to build up anticipation. You need to paint the picture clearly. Then there needs to be an unexpected twist or turn of events.

As I explain at the start of the next chapter, when you are speaking, a good way to start a talk is, before saying anything, to begin with, "Let me take you back to…" This type of start typically gets someone's attention.

Think about the difference a start can make to the same story. "I waited and waited as the minutes became hours. At last my doctor called me. I needed to come in immediately to discuss the test results. The next day, at 9:58 a.m., I was sitting in his office. He opened the report. I was fearful of the news." This builds anticipation. An alternate way to start the story, which is factual and doesn't build interest or anticipation, is as follows: "My doctor told me that I had colon cancer."

Peter Legge suggests that you sometimes want to set up a story to make sure you have everyone's attention. For example, you could say: "The story I'm about to share can change your life. It is simple, yet profound. You should listen carefully."

One great storyteller is Larry C. Farrell. Larry tells stories about people he has personally interviewed or thoroughly researched to get the best entrepreneurial examples of a particular practice and then he creates a real story about them. As Larry explains, "It's a super powerful technique. I've actually heard former participants, from 20 years earlier, perfectly re-tell one of my stories and say they remember the key principle or practice because they remember the story!"

Another great speaker who uses this approach is John Lennox, Professor Emeritus of Mathematics at Oxford University. He also holds an MA and DPhil from Oxford University. He has lectured extensively in North America, Eastern and Western Europe, and Australasia, on mathematics, the philosophy of science and the intellectual defense of Christianity.

He has also written a number of books on the interconnection between science, philosophy and theology. John has been a guest instructor in the Entrepreneurial Leaders Programme that I run each summer in Oxford. During one of his presentations, he told a story about sitting in on a lecture by C.S. Lewis. That got everyone's attention. C.S. Lewis has had an enormous impact on Western culture through his various writings, including The Chronicles of Narnia (over 100 million copies sold). He died in 1963. I had never spoken to anyone who had known C.S. Lewis or had any direct contact with him. John had. He explained that when he was an undergraduate student at the University of Cambridge in 1963, he attended some of the last lectures Lewis ever delivered. Lewis would enter the room, talking as he came in while removing his coat, scarf and hat as he came to the podium. At the end of the lecture Lewis would reverse the process. Still in full flow, he would put on his coat, scarf and hat and say his last words as he burst out of the double doors. No time for Q&A! It was a memorable opportunity for John to hear an influential thinker, and as a story, it hooked everyone.

The bottom line: think of your opening hook as getting out of the starting gate. You typically have a better chance of succeeding if you are off to a good start.

LAW #4: Put considerable effort into your opening to establish a "hook" that communicates right from the outset that you are worthy of everyone's attention.

A.5: STORY TIME

Let me take you back to Hong Kong in 1985. I had just touched down at Kai Tak Airport, with no job, no prospects, and only a few months' worth of money. My dream was to work for a law firm in Hong Kong doing work for international companies wanting to enter the China market. At that time, China had only recently opened up to the outside world. In 1979 Deng Xiao Peng announced the "Open Door Policy" to bring in Western investment, but not ideas. As he famously said, "When you open the door, the flies come in."

Have you ever wanted to pursue a dream—your dream—that others thought was preposterous? Have you ever experienced rejection and embarrassment in the pursuit? Do you realize that taking the risk and pursuing your dream makes all the difference, and will separate you from others? Your character will dwarf your competence. Let me explain how I experienced this.

I had just graduated from McGill Law School. I wanted to get to Hong Kong and start looking for a job and an opportunity right after graduation, so I booked my flight. My only contact was an acquaintance from law school, who had gotten hired in Hong Kong. He said I could stay at his flat in Pok Fu Lam.

I knew virtually nothing about Hong Kong. Before I left, I remember having met with one of my aunts. She asked, "Is Hong Kong an island?" I said I didn't know. So, she cracked open a massive atlas, weighing in at about 20 pounds and covering a coffee table. Lo and behold, I discovered that Hong Kong was comprised of Victoria Island, Kowloon and the New Territories. I was planning to go somewhere and I didn't even know what it was. Being only 25, long on enthusiasm and short on research, I was ready to pursue my passion.

A number of factors prompted a passion within me. I had read a number of articles about China "opening up," and was excited to explore a new region of business. I was also excited to travel to a different part of the world and experience a new culture.

Before leaving for Hong Kong, I didn't quite realize how preposterous my plan actually was. I had "The Five No's" going against me, in homage to China's Communist Party ubiquitous slogans. No, I was not yet a member of the legal profession. No, I had no experience in a law firm. No, I didn't speak a word of Chinese. No, I had never been to China. No, I knew nothing about Chinese law. I'm not even sure if at that point I knew how to use chopsticks.

My plan was to land, head to my friend's place, and then start looking for a job at a law firm. Of course, in the days before the Internet, the only way to do that was what would now be viewed as "the old school method": pounding the pavement and meeting people.

I had printed out copies of my resume, along with an article I had written on Canadian companies in China which was to be published in the *McGill Law Journal*. I began my quest. I had a directory of major law firms, and I went to the area called "Central" and located office towers with the most law firms.

I would show up at the reception desk and introduce myself politely, say I was looking for a job, and ask to speak to the managing partner. I remember to this day the looks I received from the receptionists. Most were dismissive. Some were pitying. Others didn't want to get too close, in case some ineptitude would rub off on them.

I was quite a sight. Since I had only recently graduated from law school, I had a limited wardrobe. Most law students have one suit: the one that they wear to interviews. I was no different. Since I had been studying in Montreal, my outfit was meant for a colder climate. I remember that I had slacks and a "Harris Tweed," which is a bit thick. I later learned that in Hong Kong there are "summer suits" and "winter suits," but at the time, I was stuck knocking on the doors of law firms in my Harris Tweed, sweating profusely in the 100% humidity and 95°F heat.

On top of all that, I wear glasses. I should have had contact lenses; I was sweating so much the glasses kept sliding down my nose. I also had two days of beard growth. It wasn't intentional. I had an electric shaver and I didn't realize that there was a different voltage in Hong Kong, which meant my North American shaver didn't work. I thought it was better to start looking for a job before looking for a razor.

So, I began going up and down buildings and in and out of impressive lobbies. Every day I would have my sights set on a few firms. After a couple of weeks and having offered my CV numerous times, I was beginning to wonder if this was going to work. But I hadn't yet exhausted all possibilities, so I pressed on. Just when I was on the verge of giving up, I got a break—as we often do when we combine focus, determination and persistence.

I came to the office of a firm called Johnson, Stokes & Master. It was the largest law firm in Hong Kong, with five floors and two buildings in Central. They had been in Hong Kong since the early days of British colonization, and they represented the "who's who" of major banks and trading companies.

I approached the reception desk and asked to speak to the managing partner. The receptionist asked, "Do you mean Mr. Peter Thompson?"

I responded, "Yes."

"Do you have an appointment?"

"No."

"Do you have a business card?"

I did, actually, have a business card, and therefore, to paraphrase Descartes, I was. In Hong Kong, without a business card you don't exist. Before leaving home I had business cards printed. My father was a general contractor, and his company was called "Edgewood Construction Ltd." I had a company card made up calling myself "Vice President—International." I thought it sounded quite impressive.

I handed her the card. "What is the purpose of your visit?" she asked.

"I would like to, uh, discuss doing business in Hong Kong."

The receptionist said, "Please wait a moment." So, I sat in the ornate reception area admiring the dark wood paneling, the black leather furniture and artwork. I thought to myself that the worst that could happen was that I would get asked to leave. That would be embarrassing, but I would simply move on, and I would likely never see them again.

The receptionist reappeared after what seemed like an eternity and said, "Mr. Thompson will see you now." Now, I was really nervous.

I still remember being led down a long corridor to Mr. Thompson's office. We eventually arrived, and it was right out of a movie set: large, finely decorated, with all the trappings of status and success. He was quite friendly when we met, perhaps buying the idea that I was a prospective client who washed up on his shores. I had a seat. "Yes, I would like some tea, thank you."

He began to ask some questions. "What brings you to Hong Kong? What are your plans for your business?"

After a few questions and vague responses, I thought that I should fess up, end the charade, and tell him why he was wasting his time with me. I said, "Sorry, I'm here because I am looking for a job." At that point I pulled out my CV and the article I had written.

The expression on his face changed. He accepted my paperwork, and, with his reading glasses perched on the end of his nose, looked down and gave it a quick glance. He said, "I'll pass this information on to our partnership secretary. Thank you."

As the meeting came to an abrupt end and I walked down the hallway, I took a good, long look, thinking that this was the last time I would ever see this office.

I was ready to continue my search. The next day, Day 27, I took up the gauntlet again. At the end of the day, however, I received a phone message from Johnson, Stokes & Master asking me to come in as soon as possible. It turns out that the firm had just decided to beef up its China department and they were about to start looking for junior lawyers in support. On Day 28 I was called in for an interview with a senior lawyer.

They offered me the standard first year lawyer compensation. I started work on Monday, exactly 30 days after I arrived.

I had landed a job with the largest law firm in Hong Kong. If they had advertised they would have gotten many great applications and far better candidates. But me showing up on their doorstep, with availability and gumption, made their decision easy—they could give me a chance and save themselves the long process of searching for someone to hire.

The job turned out to be a turning point for me. I had a great job. I had a full-time assistant. There was a tea lady who would come by regularly with her libations. The firm had regular parties and sponsored events, such as the Rugby 7's and the Dragon Boat Races. They had a beachfront condo on an outlying island. They had a company "junk" and boat boys constantly at the ready. The partners would invite me along for the short walk to the Hong Kong Club for long lunches. I filled out the table of 8 (that's when I learned at lunch that it is better to have both a red and a white wine to reduce the stress of choosing between the two).

On the work side, I was sent to China a number of times. The firm hired a language tutor for me. I was doing research on Chinese law and by the end of my year I was able to publish two books on Chinese business law. I stayed at the firm for one year before heading back to Canada to do my articling year, then do a Masters of Law at Columbia University, and then return to Hong Kong. But that year ended well.

But where did it start? With a dream. What is your dream? Every cliché you have heard is true. My actions began with a thought, and the passion to persevere. I could have considered the risk and not gone. I could have given up after many rejections, but my persistence paid off. That year in Hong Kong led to a series of positive outcomes that impact my life's trajectory to this day.

I tell this tale at some length to make the point that stories are vital to the way people learn. Great public speakers have great stories that they know how to tell to bring forth emotion and make a connection with the audience. The above is one of my stories. I have told it many times. I will emphasize or remove various bits depending upon the audience. Since it is my story, it is easy for me to remember and to tell extemporaneously and with emotion. You need to find your own stories, and learn to tie them in with a clear lesson.

LAW #5: We all learn through stories and retain information best when it's part of a story. Learn to tell a story well, and integrate it into the point of your presentation in order to communicate your message effectively.

A.6: IT'S NOT ABOUT YOU

If, at your core, you truly believe that the event where you have been invited to speak is about you and that you are bigger than the event, "then, Grasshopper, it is not yet time for you to leave."

When you begin public speaking, the focus on you as a speaker tends to go to your head. The organizers of the event are promoting you as the speaker. You are a minor celebrity. People are coming to hear you, yes, you.

A mark of an inexperienced speaker is that they think it is about them. I have worked with the world's leading speakers. How do you get there? You focus on how you can help organizers achieve their purposes. Whenever I do any form of public speaking, I always remind myself that I am not bigger than the event; rather, the event is bigger than me. I am there to fit into the organizer's program—not the other way around. Peter Legge, as one of North America's top speakers, will always ask an event organizer, "How can I help you?" Further, if you ask him to speak for a certain length of time, he will do that almost down to the second. It's not about him.

Take another example. This speaker was an Ivy League graduate, an employee with a global consulting firm, a hi-tech entrepreneur and investor, and a best-selling author. With all these credentials, he was also one of the lowest-rated speakers I have ever had (based on response forms I received).

Why was he rated so poorly?

This man was presenting at an ELO meeting for about 25 high level executives from around the world. To be clear, this program attracts very successful entrepreneurs and business leaders. For example, one member is the executive chair of a global manufacturer with 15,000 employees and $4 billion in revenue. Another is a Southeast Asian entrepreneur with development projects in the hundreds of millions of dollars. Yet another headed up an international non-profit organization with 50,000 employees worldwide, as well as numerous successful large-scale entrepreneurial endeavors. The group was a self-confident, low-key crowd. Nobody came with anything to prove. Discussions were quite cordial, though insightful and grounded in considerable high-level experience.

I introduced our guest presenter fully, and people had seen his bio earlier. Nevertheless, he spent most of the time interrupting his session with various remarks about his accomplishments. He was so ingratiating that he became a living stereotype. Some people coughed. Others went to the bathroom and did not come back until the session was over. I thought that they were on their way home. The speaker was not merely excessive, he was downright narcissistic. He had an incredible desire to try to prove himself. His tactics might have worked with impressionable bumpkins, but no one at that particular meeting was fooled. The proof came out in the assessments at the end of the course. It was as bad as I thought. He scored the worst—by a long shot—of any presenters I had had over 15 years.

The bottom line is that, the more you boast about your credentials, the more you reveal yourself to be inexperienced, insecure or self-centered. Let others, such as the event or program coordinator, tout your credentials for you. No one will be impressed if you say it yourself. In fact, you will simply alienate yourself from your audience, and they will get increasingly skeptical, wary of believing anything you say. By the end of the session detailed above, most attendees weren't sure they could believe anything the speaker said.

As a person, you don't want to be self-centered. As a speaker, you don't want to be self-centered, either. A speaker's traits are often magnified from the podium. People will pick up on things indicating that you are self-centered, from your attitude, abuse of the podium, or going overtime.

While I have explained the law above, there are some nuances. You may be put in situation where you need to sell yourself and your product to some degree. In these situations, the platform is an opportunity to sell. Be careful doing so, because if you spend too much time talking about yourself, you won't be spending enough time delivering value.

Stefanie Hartman shared with me some of her insights on how to balance not being self-centered and yet selling yourself and your product or service effectively. She explained, "I fully understand that it is helpful, and often necessary, for speakers to provide context for their experience to validate their expertise, and generally when it's done with the goal of offering solutions, it is seen as exactly that and quite helpful for the audience." Savvy audiences, however, can also identify the "look at awesome me" speaker who is simply getting a kick out of the spotlight. Stefanie's tip: if you are a leader that is comfortable in your own skin, and remember that your presentation is not about you and script it accordingly, then you can trust the audience to embrace your positive intention.

Stefanie also shared an insight about crafting your presentation for your listener, not yourself: "As someone who has earned a reputation as a top-selling speaker, and who creates products and courses for other speakers to sell, I can emphatically state for a fact the falsehood of increasing monetary gain by holding back solutions during your presentations. Think about it this way: if your presentation or your 'free' product offers nothing of value, then the audience can (often rightly) assume that your paid solution will be just as empty."

Stefanie's solution was to include a section of "key takeaways" in her presentations to help her listeners achieve results. Stefanie told me she started offering these takeaways early on, which not only provided a surprising amount of financial gain, but also helped her shake off her early day nerves!

LAW #6: Remember the context of the event where you are speaking, and always focus on how you can help the organizers or the audience achieve their objectives.

A.7: STRUCTURE & SYMMETRY

Does your presentation have a clear thesis and purpose, structure and symmetry, or is it like a body without a skeleton?

One of the key aspects of any presentation is structure. Structure is one of the 10 key points in the Public Speaking Laws of Success Scorecard® (see Appendix). I have listened to thousands of presentations and worked with thousands of students, and one of the most important aspects of helping everyone succeed is structure.

Part of a well-structured presentation is symmetry. When you have a symmetrical structure, you can ensure that everything is well-balanced between the introduction, body and conclusion. For example, in a twenty-minute presentation, your introduction should be 1–2.5 minutes, and your conclusion should be 2.5 minutes. Many presenters get sideswiped coming out of the gate with a 5 minute long introduction. That's way too long. Misusing your time will result in a rushed or inadequate final point and conclusion.

It all starts with a title. Ask yourself: what is the title of your presentation? Does it make sense? Is it clear? Is it engaging? The biggest challenge is often that the title is not well thought out. Maybe the talk doesn't relate to it—it seems catchy, but doesn't truly reflect the substance. You need a good, clear title. If you are doing a presentation on sales and want to use the mnemonic of K—E—Y, you could make the title something like, "Three Keys to Sales Success." A poor title would be something like, "Have You Wondered About How to Improve Sales?"

The title is not the place to pose a question—that is part of the hook during your presentation. Think in terms of making it simpler for people to remember your talk. Are they going to remember the question? That doesn't help them remember the answers you taught them. On the other hand, "Three Keys to Sales Success" is easy to remember and ties into K—E—Y; it becomes a frame the audience can use to remember your points.

You need to explain the reasoning for your title in the introduction to your talk. Think it as having a thesis as the title. This sounds somewhat obvious, but I have listened to many presentations that had a poorly-constructed title, which wasn't referred to in the introduction, wasn't explained, and left you with no idea about the main point of the presentation.

Next, make it clear how you will go about explaining your main points. Go through each of the points in a balanced and methodical fashion. The first point is... second... third... Conclude with a story that illustrates your main argument very well. When you share the story, tie in the three main points, add a closing inspirational or insightful quote, and Bob's your uncle. In this manner, you make listening easy for an audience. You communicate clearly. You lead them through the process. They know what's coming, and they can gauge the time.

Another fundamental point is that muddled thinking will result in a muddled presentation. It is hard to communicate clearly if one hasn't thought out one's presentation. When I taught at a business school at a university, I always emphasized that logic and structure make it easy for people to understand and follow along. If people need to work hard to figure out what you are trying to say, then they will tune out.

On the other hand, I still remember a presentation I heard at McGill Law School about 35 years ago. The speaker was Peter Hogg, a visiting constitutional law professor and widely-published author. After he was introduced, he said something like: "In the next 45 minutes I will be speaking about the 10 most important aspects of constitutional law. The first one is..." and away he went. He then went through each point, finished on time, and did exactly as expected. He wasted not a word. We all paid rapt attention. He was so clear you could taste it.

All you need to know to write a presentation can be summed up in a six-word maxim: think clearly, write clearly, speak clearly.

If you cannot think clearly, you are doomed. Organize your thoughts in a coherent and logical fashion. Then use your discipline to express yourself clearly in written form. As you write out your thoughts you are looping back to the thinking part and refining your work. Only after you've done both of these things are you in a position to speak clearly. You cannot speak well unless you have been able to think clearly and then to articulate those thoughts.

One of the best examples of a structured presentation that I have experienced by a non-professional speaker was by Lord Robert Edmiston. "Lord Bob," as he preferred to be called, was a billionaire based out of the UK who, at the time of his presentation, was also a member of the House of Lords (he subsequently resigned voluntarily). He was an accountant by training and a no-nonsense straight shooter, but remained dignified and diplomatic by nature. Of course, when someone is a billionaire, a major philanthropist, and a member of the House of Lords, you are naturally interested in what they have to say, and his perfect British accent was good for ten bonus IQ points. He was our keynote speaker and the recipient of our "Entrepreneurial Leaders Award." In the run up to the event, he had asked a number of questions about his presentation. I told him that attendees would be very interested in his personal story. They would want to understand a bit about his business, and then hear some of the lessons he learned.

When his presentation time arrived, it went very well. He got up and said he was pleased to be there, thanked various people, and then said the following: "I will describe a bit about how I started and grew my business. I will then share ten lessons I have learned." He did exactly what he said. When he described his own business experiences, it provided context and credibility. He then went through his ten lessons one by one. Lord Bob's presentation had a great structure, it was easily to follow, it was engaging and it was effective.

Lord Bob had very good pacing. He was comfortable in his own skin, but he didn't try to be a comedian. He was a very successful entrepreneur, not a public speaker by trade, but he was factual and informative.

Of course, what Lord Bob did sounds so obvious. Follow the instructions, have a basic structure, and deliver the goods.

An unclear mind cannot deliver a clear presentation. Your job as a speaker is to organize your thoughts into a clear and concise argument. Otherwise, your presentation can be visualized as a string of bullet points under a general heading. Without the scaffolding of a good talk, you merely have a collection of hard-to-remember points. This is not an effective way to communicate. Of course, it takes greater effort to sift through arguments, prioritize and categorize them, and then present them in a succinct manner. This, though, is what separates the good speakers from the mediocre ones. All of the time that is invested in building a good structure will pay back a manifold return.

Is this a difficult law to follow? No. At a base level, even if you have very little experience with public speaking, you can succeed simply by thinking through the main points and structure. Think carefully about your thesis, the supporting points, relevant examples and a great conclusion.

LAW #7: Good structure and symmetry are critical to delivering an effective presentation.

A.8: ROOMS FOR IMPROVEMENT

How could the same presenter come across in one location as a bore and in another—with essentially the same presentation—get rave reviews? Since I organize conferences in various cities around the world, and occasionally use the same speakers at different locations, I learned a valuable lesson by accident.

We hold our ELO events at hotel ball rooms and occasionally convention centers. This particular year, the only venue available was a convention center. Convention centers are typically large, cavernous spaces, with high ceilings and sliding partition walls. They resemble airport hangars. You could have multiple football games going at once in that much space. They are blandness personified, essentially devoid of character. This particular year the hotels were all filled up, and we were simply glad to get any space at all.

We had an event for three hundred people. The convention center space could be partitioned into individual "halls" for groups of maximum two hundred and fifty people. We made the decision to get two sections of the ballroom, planning to host our expected three hundred people in a space that could fit five hundred. I didn't know any better, and I was assured by the convention center staff that the tables could be arranged suitably.

When I arrived at the venue on the day of the event, I was immediately struck by how lifeless it felt. To work with the space, the convention staff had spread us out. There was a twenty-foot distance between the podium and the first row of attendees. The tables were spread out more than normal, and, because of the size of the room, there was still a lot of room around the perimeter of our gathering. We were like a basketball court superimposed on a football field. The high ceilings, about 30 feet above, seemed to make the room bigger, us smaller, and the empty feeling stronger. The room felt lifeless.

I had known this evening's first speaker for several years. He is an engaging, charming, and very personable speaker, and an excellent storyteller with a great sense of humor. He made his way to the podium. I sat near the front, silently congratulating myself on what a great job I did to get him as a speaker.

His talk fell flat. He seemed like he was talking to himself. His jokes and stories received virtually no response. His speech nosedived! He was so far removed from the front row and the rest of the audience that there was no personal connection, and although we had big screens to magnify his presence, his energy could not be transmitted via the screens, and he looked like a tiny figure in a massive room. The room felt lifeless, and all his enthusiasm could not fill it.

I was puzzled at the time. I didn't realize how much impact the venue had had. I thought that perhaps he just didn't resonate with our particular crowd. However, the impact of the room became abundantly clear when I had him speak at another one of our events.

This time the venue was a hotel. He was speaking in the afternoon session. We expected about 175 people for our afternoon sessions, and there was only room for 175 in the venue. The room had an average ceiling height of about twelve feet. The tables were quite close together and people had to navigate carefully to get to their seats. The front row of tables was within a few feet of the speakers. The podium was raised by only one foot, so the speakers felt like they were part of the crowd.

The room was jam-packed, and people were speaking loudly at the breaks so that they could be heard over one another. It was crowded and full of energy. There was a buzz. The speaker could literally reach out and, with one step, shake hands with the people in the front tables. We had a screen to show the PowerPoint, but it wasn't necessary to show the speaker, because he was so close that everyone could see the look on his face.

The room felt alive. When people laughed it was contagious and it reverberated off the walls. It felt like a familiar gathering, with a unified crowd feeding off its own energy. When the speaker got up to deliver his message, I could see instantly that the reception was different.

The speaker's stories were engaging, and his punch lines hit the mark and resonated with people. His personal charm filled the room. The outcome was so different to me that it was striking. This was an epiphany. It was like I unwittingly did an experiment stretching out over two years, two cities, and two venues. I felt good—given my earlier miscue, though, I wasn't patting myself on the back, but shaking my head.

If you are organizing your own session, be very careful about the room dynamics. Create an environment in which the room works for you, rather than against you. If you are a speaker, then ask the right questions leading up to the event. Your presentation—which might be great—could be dramatically undermined by the room dynamics. There are rooms for improvement.

LAW #8: Always be mindful of the space in which you're presenting. The venue can dramatically impact your audience's response, so make sure the room assists, rather than hinders, your presentation.

A.9: KNOW YOUR AUDIENCE

Pat Williams has a unique life story, and is a walking lifetime achievement award. He is a co-founder of the Orlando Magic and was named to the Orlando Magic's Hall of Fame as a member of its inaugural class in 2014. He has completed 58 marathons, including the Boston Marathon 13 times, and is the author of over 100 books. Pat retired in 2019 from a career that spanned more than 56 years, including over 30 years with the Orlando Magic and 51 years in the NBA. Pat and his wife, Ruth, are the parents of 19 children, 14 of whom are adopted from abroad, and the grandparents of 18 grandchildren and counting.

On top of all these accolades and accomplishments, Pat is among the most polished and professional public speakers that I have ever worked with—and a great guy. He was the recipient of my organization's "Entrepreneurial Leaders Award" in Toronto several years ago. He taught me one very important public speaking law of success.

First, though, let me take you back to the run up this particular event. You never quite know what to expect before working with a top speaker. Will they be arrogant? Will they be self-centered? After all, everyone is coming to hear them. However, it turns out that Pat was a pleasure to work with, and I enjoyed his keen sense of humor.

What struck me most with Pat, though, was that he asked a lot of detailed questions about the event. I found that this was one of the things that made him so good. We had gone back and forth in the months prior to the event regarding various details. When he arrived in Toronto the day before the event, we had dinner at the hotel restaurant to go over any final loose ends. I remember two questions he asked—and they contributed greatly to his success.

First, he wanted to confirm the general interest of the audience in sports, since that consumed much of his background and was clearly the wellspring of his stories. He said, "What if I talk about basketball, and go into detail about both US university teams and professional NBA teams?" Now, this was before the Raptors became NBA champions and the toast of Toronto. I said, "Yes, basketball is important, but nothing tops hockey. Canada is ice—and hockey."

I remember the look on his face like it was yesterday. He went bug-eyed. He couldn't believe it. He thought he had left civilization in the rear view mirror. In the US, hockey is important… right after football, baseball, basketball, roller derby, bowling, and competitive eating. Joey Chestnut may be more popular than Wayne Gretzky. I told him the top billing goes to the hapless Maple Leafs (and then clarified that they were from Toronto, not Hapless). "If a Maple Leaf player blew his nose too loudly, that would be fodder for media speculation as to whether a strained nostril would impact his performance," I said. Pat accepted my counsel and understood that he would need to work hockey into his presentation.

He then asked another great question. "Who is Toronto's greatest hockey rival?"

I thought to myself, *he doesn't know?* "It's the despised Montreal Canadiens, of course. They have broken Torontonian hearts more often than Shaquille O'Neal has missed free throws." Montreal is the most storied franchise in the NHL, having won the Stanley Cup a record 24 times. Toronto has won Lord Stanley's silver chalice 16 times, but has been on the skids and in a rebuilding program for over 50 years. No matter how Montreal or Toronto are doing in the standings, their games are fiercely contested for annual bragging rights. Pat understood.

The next day, we got to showtime. The crowd was ready. I introduced Pat, knowing that with a polished presenter, I could sit down and relax. From the second he got started, Pat was an absolute master in terms of storytelling, the timing of jokes, and interacting with the audience. It was like watching public speaking poetry in motion, or Karl Malone on a basketball court. He sprinkled in local references, so he didn't seem like he had come from afar. He showed respect for the crowd and the location. He quickly bonded with 300 new friends.

Then he launched into the kind of story you know is going to end in a punchline, and someone is going to be the butt of the joke. The anticipation was building, and he stretched out the story until people could barely restrain their laughter. Finally, his story reached its crescendo, and the buffoons of the piece were revealed: "The Montreal Canadiens!" The room instantaneously broke into a loud and prolonged roar of laughter. Pat had absolutely nailed it.

I was sitting in the front row, no more than a few feet from Pat when he delivered the punch line. As the laughter cascaded throughout the room, the look on his face was that of a cat that just swallowed not one, but two canaries. Without being familiar with hockey, the Montreal Canadiens, the Toronto Maple Leafs, or their storied 100-year old rivalry, Pat had delivered a great line like someone born in Toronto, by being prepared and asking questions.

The moral of the story? No matter how good you are (or you think you are), the best in the field are always prepared to ask the right questions. With respect to your own presentation, make sure you do your homework. Connect with organizers far enough in advance to ask questions and tailor your presentation accordingly. Find out what might work and what wouldn't. What would resonate with the audience? Who was last year's speaker (if you are speaking at an annual event)? What type of people will be in the audience? What can they relate to? If you are coming from out of town, are there particular aspects of the city or place you could refer to, such as location institutions or landmarks? By asking these questions, you will be able to resonate well with your audience.

The purpose of asking questions is to avoid certain assumptions you may be making about an event or an organization, which will undermine your effectiveness. For example, I founded Entrepreneurial Leaders Organization and we have annual "ELO Forums." Speakers sometimes assume that they are coming to speak to a room full of entrepreneurs and business owners. One might think so, from the name, but that's not actually the case. The core of our audience will be entrepreneurs and business owners, but a lot of our attendees are invited by entrepreneurs looking to fill a table of 10 at the event. We also get leaders of non-profit organizations at our events who want to be more entrepreneurial and innovative. Lastly, we get a general smattering of professionals and others who simply are interested in the topic. The outcome is that I instruct speakers not to say things like, "it's great to be in a room full of entrepreneurs," or "us entrepreneurs know to do this." We emphasize that we focus on entrepreneurial principles that are useful for everyone, rather than entrepreneurs as individuals.

LAW #9: Do your homework to know your audience. Ask the right questions. Prior private preparation facilitates public success.

A.10: BIG MO

In a sporting event, momentum (technically known as "Big Mo") is something everyone wants on their side. When you have it, nothing can stand in your way of scoring that goal or reaching the finish line. If you don't have Big Mo, you don't stand a chance. Like playing sports, a higher-level skill for speakers is the concept of pace and managing the momentum of a presentation.

These concepts are important for a presentation, whether it is 5 minutes or an hour long. A speaker must always go at a pace that is appropriate to the parameters provided.

If you are doing a short presentation, say 5 minutes or less, then perhaps you will focus on one main point and provide one story or example clearly related to that point. By doing so, you make it clear that you have enough time to share and explain one key thought. You can then go at a comfortable, unhurried pace. When you plan properly, you have enough time to achieve your purposes. Even in a shorter presentation, you can integrate all the aspects of a great speech. You can use silence. You can pause and wait to make sure people understand your point. You want to avoid the common gaffe that is the notion that, because you have a short amount of time to present, you can discard the rules of public speaking and race through your presentation.

Momentum is an intangible quality, but something that we as listeners still sense very strongly. When momentum is well-utilized, we feel that things are heading in a clear direction. There are "positive vibes" in the room. As a speaker, you feel that the pieces of your presentation are coming together and that there will be a successful conclusion. You can see the audience reacting positively through their body language and attention. Momentum is sustained through a focused presentation, where the points keep building in a single direction. Imagine your presentation as a spotlight shining on an idea. Momentum is like a reflector around that light beam, ensuring that it is focused, rather than scattered with a dissipation of light.

The same dynamics apply to a long presentation. I have worked with a number of very well-known speakers who can deliver a 45–60 minute keynote, and at the end the audience's reaction is still, "What, it's over already?! That felt like 5 minutes."

How do they manage this feat? They established pace and momentum. This is a very difficult skill to master.

One master of this skill is Larry C. Farrell. Larry is the founder and chair of the Farrell Company, the world's leading firm for researching and teaching entrepreneurship. He founded the firm in 1983 and went on to do ground-breaking research into the high-growth business practices of the world's great entrepreneurs. Today, over six million people, in forty countries and across nine languages, have attended the company's programs. Over the past three decades, Larry has personally taught entrepreneurship to more individuals, organizations, and governments than any other person in the world.

Larry has a "folksy" style of speaking, and he is a master storyteller. He goes methodically at a measured pace through his presentation. You know where he is headed, and you are interested in finding out how he is going to get there. A keynote with Larry seems to go by in an instant.

When someone is going at a good pace it feels very comfortable, like wearing a favorite sweater. How can you emulate that skill? It will take time and practice, but you can get started right now. Let's say that you are doing a 60-minute presentation. Longer presentations give you more time for your introduction and conclusion, and to develop your points and go through examples in detail. You can use silence and pregnant pauses to your advantage. You can pose a question to get people's attention, and then take time to work towards the answer.

On the flip side of this, however, is that with longer presentations you need to keep momentum. You need to have people be aware of where you are heading. Imagine it like you're making a movie. There needs to be a clear plotline. You need a lead character with a problem looking for help, meeting challenges, and moving toward a final yes/no solution.

When it comes to speaking, this means there needs to be clarity. If your presentation is titled "The Five Steps for Being a Better Salesperson," then people know that they can expect five points. They also likely assume a certain amount of symmetry—that each of the points will get about equal time.

With a longer presentation you also have time for proper transition sentences. For example: "Now that I have established the first point as the foundation, let me build on that with the second point." With a longer presentation you have the opportunity to summarize and repeat organizational features as you go along.

LAW #10: Always keep Big Mo on your side through the pace and momentum of your presentation, so the audience knows where you are going and how and when you are likely to get there.

A.11: BE ENGAGING

"Hi, my name is John, and I want to be your friend." How many people could pull that opening line off with charm and sincerity? Very, very few. But, then, John C. Maxwell is unique.

John is one of the world's leading authors and speakers on leadership. He has written 30 books, primarily on leadership, which have sold about 25 million copies. One of his most recent books, called *Everyone Communicates, Few Connect*, is about the fact that talking and connecting are not the same.

How do you connect with an audience? There are many elements to consider. It has to begin deep within your soul. You need to be a person who cares for and is interested in people. That way, when you are speaking, you are not speaking *to* them or *at* them, but speaking *with* them.

John Maxwell speaks so regularly all over the world that he likely can't remember where he spoke just last month. Over the years I have heard him speak in different settings. Regardless of the context, he exudes a sense of warmth and acceptance. Despite his hectic schedule, he never seems to be in a hurry.

On a couple of occasions I have been part of small gatherings John has attended. He will show up without any fanfare. He'll enter at the back of the room and just start talking to whoever is closest when he enters. He'll be in the room for up to half an hour before anyone else knows he's there. When he is talking to someone, he absolutely "locks in." He leans forward, and he listens intently. His demeanor and persona is just as evident from the front of the room. He ambles up to the stage and makes himself comfortable. He typically uses a cocktail table and high-top chair. He looks comfortable, and makes everyone else feel that way, too.

He goes at an even pace. He uses silence exceptionally well. He looks at the audience and smiles a lot. Having interacted with him on a few occasions, I have seen that he is the real deal—what you see on the platform is what you get on the floor. He lives what he writes. He is a person who tries to connect with people in whatever time he has with them.

This public speaking law is to do what you can at the outset to connect with the audience. Adapt your pacing to let your words sink in. Be expressive, and remember: the bigger the room, the more expressive you need to be.

You don't have to say anything fancy or complicated to connect with people. You can say something like, "Hi, I'm Rob. I'm here to speak about sales. In the next hour my objective is to share my experiences to help you be more effective in your activities and double your income." You just have to say it like you mean it, and believe it. It's amazing how well someone can connect with an audience within a short amount of time.

One interesting side note is that having worked with many of the world's top public speakers, I often get asked, "What are they really like?" In other words, is there a public image that doesn't match what is projected on stage? John Maxwell is the same on stage as he is in person: warm and engaging. To some extent, your ability to connect with people as a public speaker will match your ability to connect with people on an individual basis. If you aren't genuinely interested in people, it's hard to flip a switch and suddenly pretend to be.

It can be a challenge to connect with an audience. A room full of people can sometimes seem lifeless. A crowd that has assembled to hear a speaker may have been waiting for a while, leaving people bored, fidgety, and impatient with the delay. Yours might be the session right before the coffee break, or the last session of a conference. The previous speaker may have put the audience to sleep. People may simply not be interested in your topic. What should you do in these situations?

People will be more interested in listening if you are engaging. Start looking for an audience response through the various techniques as outlined below. By being an engaging speaker, you can transform the mood of a room.

Amazingly, one person can influence a crowd of as many as 80,000! Many football teams hire professional cheerleaders or mascots for this very reason. Take "Crazy George," for instance, a cheerleader at one of the professional football games I attended. He would parade through the sections with a wild-eyed expression, adorned in team swag and equipped only with a drum and sticks. He would start in one corner of a massive stadium, getting everyone riled up and focused on him. He would then get the fans to do "the wave" (i.e., stand up in unison as they lift their arms upward and then sit down in a few seconds). He would get a couple of people at first, then part of the section, and then the rest. They would do the wave. Then he would point at the next section with the drumstick, and so on, until eventually he had the whole stadium doing the wave. One guy directed everyone's behavior and changed everyone's emotion. You can do a similar thing with your audience, using different techniques to direct their mood.

At most events, the audience members do not know one another; they are sitting among strangers, yet they are all united in terms of an interest in hearing the particular speaker or learning more about the topic. Here's another technique that is frequently used as a way of getting everyone involved. "Look to the person on the right and tell them they really need to hear this": this is a line John Maxwell occasionally uses when he speaks. It's hokey, but it works. People follow the instructions, and you can hear a lot of noise and chuckling throughout the room. It breaks the ice a bit and creates an atmosphere that everyone is doing something together.

Sometimes a speaker will be discussing a topic and then ask the audience, "By a show of hands, let me know if you think the following are important." This technique gets people's attention, and they generally participate. If they weren't paying attention before, now they need to start doing so. Similarly, sometimes a speaker will ask a question and then engage a particular person in a conversation. People typically become alert because they want to hear what the audience member is saying, and they want to be ready if they are called on next!

If you are able to engage the audience, do it, but only when it's appropriate. Engaging an audience immediately removes the barrier not only between the speaker and the audience, but among audience members. This technique can work well to break down barriers and to develop a comfort level with the speaker and the people around you. However, trying to engage an audience is a higher-level skill and takes a degree of comfort as a speaker and is not appropriate in all circumstances.

If you have a room full of senior executives and ask them to get up, stand on one leg, hop around their tables to another table and ask someone their favorite ice cream flavor, it might not go over well. You may think it is a humorous ice breaker. The audience, by contrast, may think it's infantile and pointless. They won't cooperate, and many of them will wait in a bathroom stall until the grown-ups reappear. Ultimately, though, when done right, the ability to work with a crowd shows the consummate skill of the presenter who understands the audience and is willing to engage with people.

LAW #11: As appropriate, try to engage the audience during the course of your presentation, whether through interaction, questions, polls, shows of hand, or some other form of interaction—and you can create the right crowd mood for a successful presentation.

A.12: BE PREPARED

"I am so sorry... I really don't know what I am doing." Yes, that is what the speaker said, quivering at the podium in front of hundreds of befuddled spectators. People looked like they were seeing the Elephant Man, obviously feeling embarrassed simply by being in the room. This man's company had paid $5,000 for him to have the opportunity to present his company's vision, hoping for more investment dollars from a private equity forum in the Big Apple, the finance capital of the world.

The basic concept of this event was that the organizer would gather the usual suspects, some wealthy and some pretending to be, on the premise that there might be a few good deals. The organizer would try to solicit reasonable investment opportunities, and the entrepreneurial hopefuls would pay for the privilege of getting to speak in front of these would-be investors. The companies would be left to their own devices to shine—or not—at the appointed hour. It was a bit like a private equity beauty contest.

The organizer's venue of choice was the Yale Club. Not quite the Harvard Club, but still very classy. The room, however, was not designed for presenters. Imagine a bowling alley—this room was about as wide and only slightly shorter. It was long and narrow, and there wasn't enough space to set up the podium centrally, so it had to be at one end of the long room. Already, this was a bad start.

As we in the audience listened to a parade of aspiring entrepreneurs of varying quality, we had our next hopeful make his way to the podium. He wasn't exactly projecting an air of confidence, but we tried to keep an open mind. As he bumbled through his presentation, though, he did many of the things not to do when delivering a public presentation.

He began reading his presentation, head down, barely looking at the PowerPoint. His voice was monotonous. His explanations were unclear.

He spoke too fast. His presentation slides were far too detailed, with microscopic font too small to be read by anyone beyond the first few rows. It wasn't his fault that the room was so long and narrow, but he could have checked the room out earlier in the day and adjusted his presentation accordingly.

To top it all off, he ended up running out of time. The investor forums and other groups are strict about time, so with that, he was over and out.

The entire presentation from start to finish was an unmitigated disaster. The company paid a fee to be there, another fee for the time of the person delivering the presentation, and the cost of travel expenses. It got no results. The presentation was so bad that people forgot about trying to understand the speaker and were simply showering pity upon him. Not only was it not a useful investment: it was downright counterproductive. The person and the company came off looking incompetent—clearly not a company to invest in.

This person and company invested money in the event and they should have been prepared. They weren't and it cost them dearly. It sounds so obvious that a person should be ready before hitting the stage—but, if so, then why don't people do it?

If you are participating in an event, do it well or not at all. For starters, a person or a company needs to decide if they have the time and energy to properly prepare for a presentation. Make sure that you are aware of what is involved in doing well at an event. Investor presentations at private equity fundraising events, for instance, can be quite detailed in terms of preparation and presentation. You will also be dealing with a crowd that has seen many presentations, and your audience will tune out very quickly if they sniff telltale signs of a poor presentation. If you don't prepare, it will backfire.

LAW #12: Be prepared, or don't proceed. Otherwise, your presentation will be counterproductive.

A.13: BE PRESENT

Survivor, *Shark Tank*, *The Apprentice*, and *The Voice*: Mark Burnett is the originator and producer behind these and many other top Hollywood shows. He is, at the time of writing, the chair of MGM Worldwide Television Group, and is regarded as one of Hollywood's leading producers. Beyond that, he is among the best of hundreds of well-known speakers I have hosted.

A few years ago, Mark Burnett agreed to be a speaker at one of the ELO forums, hosted in Vancouver. He was initially planning to come with his wife, actress Roma Downey, star of the famous TV series, *Touched By An Angel*. Mark and Roma were going to participate with me in a Q&A during our afternoon session, and then Mark would do the evening keynote on his own. We began promoting Mark and Roma's participation in our conference many months in advance. We worked with his handlers on the format of the panel and all the sundry details.

Then a family situation arose, and Roma wasn't able to make it, instead needing to do a video conference interview. Mark also faced some challenges making it to Vancouver. He's a busy guy with lots of deadlines. At first, he was going to come the night before our event. Then, when that didn't work, he was going to come the morning of our event so he could join the Q&A in the early afternoon. The time frame kept shrinking, until he was scheduled to come later that same day and do the afternoon Q&A at around 4 p.m. There was very little margin of error left. We had sold tickets to the afternoon session (1:00–5:30 p.m.) on the basis that he was going to be there, and at this point, I was getting quite nervous as to whether he would actually be able to headline the event.

As it turned out, all of my concerns were unfounded. He showed up at the hotel shortly before the afternoon Q&A. He did a great job, answering all questions with grace and good humor. He clearly conveyed that he was glad to be part of our event. From the moment he arrived, he was completely committed to doing a great job, not getting distracted, and helping us with our event.

His evening keynote was also outstanding, with great humor, insight, and emotion. He recounted growing up in east London, later following his dream to work in the USA. He was a great speaker, and had obviously told his story many times previously. He was very likable. People could sense his enthusiasm for adventure and his desire to make a difference. After his evening keynote, a lot of people wanted to speak with him. He didn't hastily exit stage right. Instead, he was unfailingly courteous and polite. He talked to every last person and gave them his full attention. I was standing nearby and I could hear that many questions and comments could have been given short shrift, but he stayed attentive.

After the presentation, my most vivid memory is of him being the last person, apart from myself and my wife, to exit the hotel ballroom—over an hour after the event had ended. The hotel staff had already rolled away most of the tables and stacked virtually all of the chairs. It was close to 10:30 p.m. when he headed up to his hotel room. He was leaving early the next morning. As we were leaving the empty ballroom, I complimented him on his willingness to engage with people at length. He told me, "I never want anyone to say that I didn't have time for them." As we parted company and I watched him go up the escalator and back to his room, I thought about the fact that I would likely never see him again, and by the end of the week he would likely not even remember this event, but he still honored a commitment to deliver as promised, keep his integrity, and built goodwill.

The most important lesson I learned from Mark was to "be present." Once he was in town, he was tuned in and entirely focused on our event. He was clearly committed to doing his best and giving us his full attention. He wasn't looking past us to his next event. He was doing us a favor by joining the conference, and was only in Vancouver for less than 24 hours, but he was entirely committed to the present task at hand. Having worked with hundreds of speakers, I can confirm that, for many speakers, your event is clearly just one more pit stop on their tour. They go through the motions, but a speaking mannequin could do the job just as well.

A good speaker doesn't focus on the next event. Instead, focus on the people and the event where you are. They are the most important audience that you have.

LAW #13: Whenever you do a presentation, "be present" and in the moment. Be committed to the task at hand.

A.14: GOLDILOCKS

One approach to public speaking is "reading it," or rigidly reading out your presentation script. The other extreme, "winging it" with a free-flowing, extemporaneous stream of consciousness, is not good, either. Both of these are bad ideas, and somewhere in the middle, as with Goldilocks, is generally just right. Let me give an example of the two extremes.

My heart sank the moment I saw this speaker get to the podium and pull out a pile of notes. Sure enough, he began to read through his notes word for word—barely coming up for air. The bulk of the time people were looking at the top of his shiny pate.

It was even worse once he hit the allotted time with no sign of slowing down. Then he went past the margin of error and well into the red zone. That's when I got up. I thought I would be discreet, so I walked to the back of the room where no one could see me. I was hoping to get his attention. No luck. His wife, realizing how badly it was going, came to join me. We both couldn't get his attention. I was literally at the back of the ballroom with his wife, gesticulating wildly, and he never looked up. After he eventually finished, considerably over time, I asked if he noticed me signaling that time was up. He said he didn't even see me! He didn't realize that he was over time. I thought, *wow, that is really out of touch.*

The tragedy of the entire episode is that this fellow has had an amazing life and business journey. He built a large international enterprise. His stories had all the potential to be riveting, but public reading made the keynote excruciatingly long and boring instead. When he was reading, he wasn't looking up and interacting with the audience. Worse yet, he couldn't see who was at the back of the room trying to save him.

This scenario is not uncommon. The bottom line: never read a presentation, except for very narrow and limited circumstances. If you are going to read out your presentation, you might as well ask someone to print and distribute it and then sit down.

In some cases, you can have detailed notes for reference as you do a specific type of presentation. Perhaps you are called upon to thank a group of people, such as sponsors, and there are 20 names, titles, and cities. You want to make sure you don't forget anyone and you don't get it wrong. That's fine. Another exception is in an academic context. I have sat through many dramatic readings of academics presenting their papers. They just get up and read the paper, looking up occasionally to make sure that people are still in the room. However, academic readings are not held to the same standards as more general public presenters.

Long ago, you learned to read. Now you need to learn *not* to read. Public reading is not public speaking. Public speaking is an entirely different mode of communication. At a conference, especially as a keynote speaker, reading from your notes is a sure way to kill your audience's interest.

At the other extreme is winging it. When you wing it, you don't have any notes—you'll just start talking. Here's an example of the perils of winging it.

I was at a municipal chamber of commerce gathering, and the featured speaker was a local fellow who had become a highly-respected astrophysicist. His talk was on some other-worldly space-time continuum. He was a leading expert in observational cosmology, cosmic microwave background radiation, submillimeter astronomy and the physics of star formation—so much so that his audience didn't know what much of it meant, but it sure sounded impressive. At least, it sounded impressive until he opened his mouth. As soon as he started speaking, things went downhill fast.

The first bad sign was that there was no title to the talk. He just started talking! That's the way it went on—he spoke extemporaneously, and proceeded in anything but a straight line. The talk went in circles, in pursuit of every rabbit trail and sidebar. He had stories to tell, but didn't know how to tell them, and ended up sharing a series of snippets. By the time he finished, the audience was applauding more because it was over than because they had enjoyed his talk. It didn't have to be this way.

Speaking extemporaneously is high-risk. You need to be quite experienced to pull it off. The idea is that when you get to the podium you will figure out what to say, as if somehow your walk to the front of the room will bring some clarity. It won't. We have all witnessed too many events where the person at the front of the room has no idea what to say, but thinks that if they talk long enough that they will eventually get to something worthwhile. You should try to avoid being in this situation.

When you're starting off in public speaking, try to strike a balance. Have a set of notes with a brief outline you can refer to. It might be as simple as having three key points. With each key point, have a story connected to it, and notes that trigger your memory as you go. You can then comfortably look up from the podium and deliver your speech. It will be just right.

LAW #14: Strike a comfortable balance of speaking extemporaneously as much as possible, with reference to an outline or presentation slides.

A.15: HUMOR IS NO JOKE

The ability to have an audience laugh at points during your presentation is a great asset. Humor makes it easier for you to connect with the audience, get your message across effectively, and have fun. However, be aware of the context. If you are going to attempt to get laughs, then be very careful about the difference between humor and "telling a joke."

First, let's look at the dynamics of telling a joke. It's like playing with fire. Telling a joke is high-risk and it can end badly. Take the following example. A number of years ago I was at a small workshop of about 50 people. There were three presenters. One of the fellows was a financial planner, and he was going to deliver a short presentation introducing his firm and its services.

He was a bit awkward at the podium, as if he was told what to do but didn't quite know how to do it. He might be a competent financial planner, but he was not a public speaker, and someone had given him some bad advice. He began by saying, "I want to tell a story…" It was instantly apparent that he was launching into a canned joke. "There was an old man with a cane, and a one-eyed guy named Fred. Fred was walking along the path and met a talking rabbit," etc. The speaker went through the paces, the joke ended, and the punchline fell flat. Our friend, now dutifully having told a joke, moved on. It proved that he didn't really know what he was doing in the realm of public speaking, and that this was going to be a long "short presentation."

Is it easy to tell a joke? No. Few people can do it well. One is my friend, Peter Legge, who can tell a joke better than most speakers I have ever heard. I think he has a natural gift, but beyond that, he has been speaking frequently for about 50 years. He also started out as a stand-up

51

comedian, and he has been working his material ever since. For him, a story needs an element of surprise and a bit of a twist at the end. It comes down to building expectation in the audience, and then timing the punch line well.

The mark of a great speaker is that, if you simply retell the joke later, it doesn't seem as funny. One of Peter's opening lines is as follows: "I'm glad to be here in this town. The people are great. You are a wonderful audience," he'll say. "The food is excellent. Everyone is hospitable. But, unfortunately, I had some challenges getting here. There was a problem with my flight."

"Oh, no," the audience will think. They can relate to his story.

"I flew Air Canada," he'll add. Everyone there will have had problems with Air Canada as various points in their lives. "They lost my baggage."

"Oh, dear, yes, we can relate. That's terrible. A tragedy," the audience will murmur.

Then comes the punchline: "It was carry-on!"

When I have seen Peter deliver that line, there has always been a burst of laughter. When I'm retelling that story and you're seeing it on paper, you might think, *really? That doesn't seem that funny*. When delivered properly, though, it is. The skill of delivery becomes obvious when you compare what it looks like on paper and how it's received by an audience in person.

You can be in the top 10% of all public speakers you ever hear without ever trying to tell a joke, so don't bother. If you are a non-professional and infrequent public speaker, stay away from trying to tell a joke. You are unlikely to pull it off. Do not tell a canned joke. Do not think you are ready to tell a joke because you bought a book on "100 Great Jokes for Public Presentations." For less experienced speakers, you can be funny by simply telling stories about some of your experiences. If people laugh, think of it as a bonus, not a goal.

Peter has spent a lifetime at his craft, so I asked him what to do if a joke falls flat. If people don't laugh, Peter advises, get ready to say something like, "I didn't think it was funny, either, but I told it to illustrate a point." Then move on to the next point. Don't let it hang.

Think of almost any famous comedian. There are so many stories of these comedians earning their chops in small venues for years on end, honing their material, learning what resonates with people, and perfecting their delivery. Even with these success stories, we only know a few of the many thousands of aspiring comedians that are practicing today. For your average public speaker, it's too risky to tell a canned joke.

Rather than telling a joke, if you want to attempt to incorporate some humor into your presentation, try sharing a story. There is a clear difference between trying to tell a joke and being funny. You can be funny by sharing a story that happened to you or sharing funny stories. That's different from telling a joke. If you want laughs, then work in some personal funny occurrences in a way that does not expect or demand laughter, but simply invites it.

Another way of getting laughs is self-deprecating humor. If you direct your humor at belittling other people and places, it's not really that funny. By contrast, you can't go wrong with self-deprecating humor. For an example, consider an accountant I once had do a presentation at a business conference. He was actually quite good. He wasn't a comedian, and he didn't try to be something he wasn't. His presentation was numbers-focused. At one point, with a glint in his eye, he paused and said something like, "that's not bad for an accountant, eh?" Everyone started laughing. He took the words out of everyone's mouths. At the end of his presentation, he came across as a competent accountant with a good sense of humor. In short, he seemed like the type of person who would be great to work with.

Lastly, you can have some quips in your repertoire that you use when the time is right. I am a Mennonite by background. Sometimes Mennonites have a reputation for being overly concerned about what others think. They are often teetotalers and very frugal, to boot. I spoke at a Mennonite business conference years ago, and while I was describing an ethical dilemma for business leaders, I paused and said that reminded me of a classic Mennonite dilemma: "free wine." There was a burst of laughter. It was the right crowd, and I mentioned it at the right time. It wasn't a canned joke. It didn't rely on the audience laughing to succeed. If it had fallen flat, that would have been fine, as I simply would have moved on.

The bottom line is that you can carefully integrate humor into your presentation. Don't start with a focus on jokes. Try to integrate humor, but don't wait for laughter—that's too high risk.

LAW #15: Don't joke around, but humor is a plus. Getting laughs is a good part of a presentation, but it's a high-risk arena. Where humor is appropriate, focus on your own personal stories.

A.16: LESS IS MORE

"**I** can make it through." The presenter was very confident when I checked that he could keep to the time provided.

I asked, "Are you sure?"

He responded again, "Yes, absolutely!"

He was an experienced speaker, traveling the world to extol the virtues of his consulting practice. He was very well-traveled, and would essentially give some variation of his core talk over and over again. I thought it was a given that he would have it down pat. He had a well-deserved reputation for being headstrong and self-centered, but I believed we could work with him anyway.

I explained to him that he had exactly 30 minutes. I reminded him that we had a tight schedule and that there were a number of other speakers throughout the day, so going overtime would mean robbing someone else of their time.

I had gotten into the habit of asking for people's presentation slides in advance of their presentations so that I could review the content. I also had a general idea of how many slides most presenters could comfortably go through in the time provided. A general rule of thumb is to have no more than one slide per minute.

Instead of 20-30 slides, this speaker came in at a whopping 60. I advised against it, but he insisted that he would get through his entire deck. I was reluctant, but I supposed that since he was an experienced presenter and was doing me a favor by speaking at our event, I would defer to him on the matter.

I introduced him very briefly, to buy him an extra minute. At the outset of his presentation, squandering precious time, he said, "Rick only gave me 30 minutes and I have a lot of slides to get through, so I'll do my best." That's a bad way to start off. Complaining about getting limited time is irrelevant to anyone in the audience, and it's an insult to the organizer. Always take ownership for your own presentation.

This experienced presenter then began to race through his slides, determined to get to the end—to complete the task—whether anyone understood his content or not. He talked very fast and skipped through much of his material. At the end of the presentation, exactly what I feared would happen, did. He ran out of time, went through way too quickly, and did himself a disservice. Later, the response forms conveyed the same message: great material, good presenter, but there was way too much material and he went too fast. He clearly had not practiced; if he had, he would have known that he could not get his presentation completed.

In the end, he did get through his slides and he was only a few minutes overtime, but his presentation felt like being in the passenger seat of a runaway race car careening down the road. People seemed out of breath when it was over. It was not his finest half hour.

The speaker should have prepared in advance with an eye on the time he had been given. In light of the time allocated, he should have limited his deck to 20-30 slides. That way, he could have gone through them at a calm pace. Instead of complaining about the agreed-upon timespan, he could have said at the outset, "Given the time I have, I will go over these core concepts; there is much more I could say, and I would be pleased to address questions later."

Usually with public speaking you will be allotted a certain amount of time to speak. Plan around those fixed parameters and give yourself a comfortable time to complete your talk (including the time needed to manage silence and pauses well). I usually recommend building in a 5-10% buffer during your practice; a practice run is typically a bit shorter than when you deliver in front of an audience. When you've practiced, it's like you are methodically building your cake according to the recipe: you know you have enough time to do so. If, on the other hand, you think you should have been allocated more time and you want to squeeze everything in before you run out of minutes, then time will be working against you.

You'll start speaking too fast, and going over points too quickly. You'll feel like you are staring at an hourglass almost out of sand.

Here is an example of how to do it well. Les Hewitt is a leadership expert and public speaker who co-authored *The Power of Focus* with Mark Victor Hansen and Jack Canfield (famous creators of *Chicken Soup for the Soul*). Les speaks regularly and has done a lot of training courses. He has also organized his own conferences, put together his own program, and handled plenty of high-profile speakers.

I was organizing an evening session and we already had a keynote speaker, but I wanted to work him into the line up. I asked him if he could do a five-minute talk about just one key point. I had another person to give a five-minute talk, and then the keynote speaker was to take the stage.

Les spoke for five minutes—almost to the second. He didn't complain about the lack of time. He never said, "if only I had more time, I could do a much better job and deliver more content." Most vividly, I remember that he had a very measured and deliberate pace. He spaced out his thoughts, and he wasn't in a hurry. It sounded the same as if he had been prepared to speak for half an hour.

When you finish comfortably on time, you convey the following:

1. You are prepared.
2. You have practised and are likely experienced.
3. You are a professional.
4. You respect the organizer's time.
5. You respect the audience's time.
6. It's not about you—you are there to contribute to the event.

For a short talk, it's important to be very well organized. Have your first few lines and your closing lines very clear. Have the framework of the talk firmly in your mind. As much as possible, memorize the talk—not so that you are speaking robotically, but so that you are flowing from one thought to the next and using words for maximum impact. In a short talk, there is no margin of error. With just one sidebar, you are 25% over your allotted time.

The bottom line: less is more. Say less, and say it well.

LAW #16: Plan your presentation carefully to ensure you can go at a comfortable pace to fill the time provided. You are communicating a message, not trying to win a contest to get through the most material in your allocated time.

A.17: TOUCH THE HEART

Failure. Tragedy. Mental health challenges. These subjects are difficult to discuss—especially from the podium.

The most powerful presentations, though, are often those that bring out emotion. As one of my friends said after a conference, the speakers he likes best "are the ones that touch my heart." The emotion of the speaker is something that the listeners can relate to and connect it to their own experiences. These shared experiences create an emotional resonance.

However, there is a difference between the emotion transferred to the audience and the emotion kept on stage with the speaker. I have seen speakers become emotional on stage while the audience is simply unmoved—and it can be like watching a train wreck. People feel more awkward than empathetic, and it doesn't impact them. They haven't connected with the speaker's experience.

On the other hand, there are examples of speakers who are able to explain an emotional situation with which people can identify. Peter Legge has told the following story a few times.

As a 12-year-old boy, Peter attended a private boys' school in England. One year, they had a sports day. Peter was not very good at running, but he tried out for the "Half Mile for Boys." Sure enough, young Peter did not make the cut for the 15 finalists. However, his parents had contributed money for the trophy for that particular race, and the headmaster informed him that because his parents had donated a trophy, he would have to put Peter in the race.

The big day arrived. Peter was the 16th entry in the slightly expanded field. The four-lap race began, and at the end of the first lap Peter was dead last. Then he passed the clubhouse turn and caught the eyes of his mother, father and grandfather. He couldn't disappoint them. He put his tiny butt in gear. At the end of the second lap, he was in tenth place. At the end of the third lap he was in fifth place. By the final lap he finished in first place. He still has the trophy to this day.

Every time Peter tells this story, it has an impact. Have you been a kid wanting to win something to make your parents proud? Have you been a parent, wanting your kids to get a boost of confidence by winning some competition? Do you like to win? Do you like that feeling of having given your all—and having come out victorious? You remember what it felt like, and Peter's story takes those emotions to the present. Part of what make Peter's stories so compelling is his transparency, sense of timing, candor, and vulnerability.

I have another example of an emotional story. Phil Vischer was a speaker at one of our ELO Forums, as well as the creator of the ground-breaking children's series, *Veggie Tales*. With the help of his wife, a college buddy, two art school grads and his church's music director, Phil landed *Veggie Tales* videos in a third of all American households with young children.

And then, at the peak of Phil's success, everything turned upside down. Phil's company, Big Idea Productions, was forced into bankruptcy in 2003. He lost his company, his characters, his dream. What he didn't lose, though, was his faith and hope. Phil found himself with a ministry he never expected—a ministry to anyone who has lost a dream. Phil has detailed the dramatic rise and fall of his dream and the lessons learned in his well-reviewed book, *Me, Myself & Bob: A True Story about Dreams, God and Talking Vegetables* (Thomas Nelson, 2008).

Phil's telling of his story at our event was quite gripping. We have all failed. We have all made mistakes. We can all relate to Phil's story. We have all lost something that we have dearly cherished. Dealing with failure is part of being in business. Things don't always work out—many times it doesn't! The challenge is to have and maintain faith when a dream is shattered—and that the focus of Phil's talks.

So, how can you "touch the heart" of your audience? This will depend, of course, on the context of your presentation. Here are some general points.

Think of something you have experienced. Perhaps it relates to some of your core relationships. For example, I have heard people share a story along the following lines.

The boy was about twelve years old at the time. There was a general store in his community, not far from where he lived, and one day he biked past it and spotted a vase. His mother's birthday was coming up, and the boy wanted to do something special for her. He had a few dollars he had gathered together from cutting grass and doing other odd jobs, so he used that money to buy the vase and gave it to his mother on her birthday. She was thrilled, and put it on the mantle, and said it would always remind her of her son's love for her, no matter where he was in the world.

As the years went by, and mother and son both aged, the vase remained on the mantle. Eventually, the boy's mother finally passed away. As the son and his siblings sorted through his mother's few earthly belongings, the son came across that birthday gift, and realized it was not that nice a vase. He took that vase, anyway, and brought it to his house. It now sits on his mantle, and it reminds him of the love that his mother had for him.

This simple story can be quite impactful. Everyone in the audience has parents. They have family. They want loving relationships. They appreciate those who have invested in them. Everyone reflects on what is important in life. The things we value don't always have a dollar value. That simple story is a reminder of those things. You can ask probing questions: "What have you done for someone important in your life? What can you do now?" Think of your own experiences. That will make your story come to life.

The above three stories include different experiences: running a race as a child; business failure as an adult; and the love between a child and a parent. Each of these stories can make an emotional connection with an audience. For any speaker, think of one of your own experiences that expresses a universal truth that will resonate with others.

LAW #17: Try to make an emotional connection with your audience by sharing important personal experiences that will resonate with your audience.

A.18: AUTHENTICITY

Authenticity is one of the most important aspects of being a great public speaker, especially when you are starting out. If you are authentic, people can relate to you, understand you, root for you, and like you. They will overlook a multitude of public speaking sins if you have this quality.

Authenticity is revealed and displayed by being comfortable in your own skin. You're not pretending to be something you aren't. "I yam what I yam, and that's all I yam," to quote the great American philosopher, Popeye the Sailor. There is no pretense; there are no airs. You may be on a podium, but you are on the same level as everyone else.

Often, authenticity is connected to vulnerability. Now, most speakers are invited to speak because they have achieved something, they have succeeded, they have built a career or a company. They are usually not invited because the sum of their life's work is a disaster with a mountain of failures. The reality is that most people prefer not to dwell on failure. At the same time, though, we all realize that we fail along the way. When a speaker works into their story the failures along the way, it often resonates with the audience. The speaker may share their financial struggles, emotional hardship, psychological stress, and the utter despair they have experienced. Often authenticity is heightened when talking about rejection and demoralizing events a speaker experienced before turning the corner.

It may make people uncomfortable to think about failure. However, this authenticity resonates; people can relate to it, and they know it to be true to their own experience. No one has an uninterrupted string of success—it's nonsense, so don't pretend otherwise.

There are other ways of being authentic. Sometimes authenticity is revealed when a person talks about things that are really important to them. Often, authenticity is heightened through a self-deprecating sense of humor, or an acknowledgement that they have received a lot of help along the way, that they aren't the greatest, or that it did in fact "take a village" to accomplish the success the speaker has experienced.

When you speak, don't try to present an image of success (or what you imagine that to be). Rather, project what you really are. Be yourself; be the real you. Just use some public speaking laws of success so that you can communicate the real you more effectively. Knowing how to communicate is not an artifice; rather, it allows the real you to emerge.

Sometimes heightened authenticity happens where people show a lot of emotion from the stage, as long as they have previously made a connection with the audience (as per the previous laws). Margo Engberg, Founder of Pinkabella Cupcakes in Seattle, shared her story at one of our ELO Forums about starting a cupcake chain.

Margo said her cupcake obsession had begun when she was a little girl. She had always looked for reasons to throw a party. When she was in college, she would go home for weekends to bake, and then bring goodies back so that she could have parties in her dorm room.

As she got older, the parties evolved into much larger events. Margo started throwing wedding and baby showers for friends, large Christmas parties, and many, many birthday parties. When her kids entered school, she realized that there were many children who could not bring treats to school on their birthday, so she decided cupcakes were something she could do for all of her children's classmates. She has been building on her passion ever since, starting a chain of cupcake stores and using proceeds from store sales to give back. She has already donated over 30,000 cupcakes to schools and foundations.

As she was explaining it, she became quite emotional and started crying. We took it as a reflection of her commitment and passion. The audience was entirely with her in both her joy and agony. She didn't hide her emotion, and her presentation had a great impact on the attendees.

This is not easy to do, however, as not everyone connects so naturally with an audience. Some people might need to work harder for the same level of perceived authenticity.

I had one client as a speaker at one of our ELO Forums. He is a great guy and very genuine. I did a Q&A with him. I was surprised when the response forms came back, showing that he didn't get very good reviews at all. Upon further reflection, I started to understand why. I had known him for many years and thus worked around his personality—I didn't even think about it anymore. But the reality was that he was a reserved individual, not a very expressive one, and he focused a lot on business without showing a lot of emotion. The way he projected from stage came across as wooden, and didn't really capture much feeling. He was looking primarily at me as the interviewer, and not connecting with the audience. He did not resonate with his listeners, so unfortunately, he did not come across as authentic to them.

Maintain a careful balance when speaking. You want to be authentic in that you want your remarks to reflect the core of what you are about. You may share things that are very important to you, or you may talk about an experience that changed the course of your career. At the same time, while being authentic, you can still strive to be polished and professional and to convey your message effectively. You want to tap into your convictions, passions, and feelings about your topic.

> **LAW #18:** Be authentic, transparent and, as appropriate, vulnerable to connect well with your audience.

A.19: FOCUS

An effective presentation requires focus and direction. There are two common challenges in this respect. One is to lose focus. The other is to go off track.

Regarding the first challenge, have you ever "lost your train of thought" or "gone blank" while speaking in public? I have, but I don't remember when. If you have ever gone there, you know you don't want to go back! Les Hewitt notes in *The Power of Focus* that, in all things both big and small, long term and immediate, you need to keep your focus. With tasks such as public speaking, it is especially vital to maintain your concentration.

Sometimes this task is easier said than done. First, let's look at how you lose focus. Most of us get bored when we do something over, and over, and over. I have a few presentations that I have done countless times in many different venues. You inevitably get better at repeated presentations, since you get to know what material resonates and what doesn't, what materials people find interesting, and so on.

I find that when I present new material I get excited, while doing the same presentations over and over gets boring. I have found that occasionally in the past my mind would "go blank." It's an odd feeling. You are standing in front of hundreds of people, and all of a sudden you have no idea what the next point is, or even what you are talking about. This can be a bit disconcerting. I have found that the key is to remain calm ("keep calm and carry on"). Start talking, and eventually you will find your way back to your key point as your mind sorts itself out.

Why do you lose your focus? Typically, it is due to familiarity with the material. It doesn't take much concentration to deliver the concepts, so your mind wanders. The best way to avoid having your mind go blank in the first place is to remind yourself of the basics: this is the same presentation, but a new audience. You can also keep the framework the same but change some examples to keep it fresh for you.

There are simple prompts you can use to make sure you can recover if your mind goes blank. You can have extra notes on the presentation screen so you can glance at it as necessary, or you can have some notes on cue cards to keep yourself on track.

The biggest challenge for me was when I was teaching at the business school of a university. Often, I would teach three successive blocks of the same class. It was very difficult to remember what I covered when I would go off-script and use spontaneous examples. I always had my class outline and textbook on hand to reference, but I would still sometimes need to ask a student, "Have I used this example already?"

The second challenge is to go off track. This can happen quite easily, especially at the outset of a presentation. Something vaguely associated with the topic of the presentation pops into the mind of the presenter, and then they go off on a tangent. They start telling a story, sometimes a very long one, which has nothing to do with the thrust of the presentation. Or, a variation of the same theme, the presenter starts telling a story as planned, but then they start to throw in too many details. Now the story has distorted their entire presentation—it's too long, convoluted, and ultimately distracting. This often happens because a person is telling a personal story from memory and simply recounting it in front of an audience. Instead of falling into this trap, remember to have a series of markers related to the story, such as key facts or lessons to draw out, even when you are familiar with your story. This kind of preparation will keep you on track

Another way to get off track is to be a bit too casual. I have experienced many a speaker who comes up to the podium to deliver a keynote at the end of a dinner. "Wow, that chicken was good. My, it was tasty. It reminds me of the best chicken I've had, which was on a trip to..." Who cares? It signals to the audience that they will need to sit through the chaff of irrelevant commentary to get to the wheat of the presentation.

I have sat through too many presentations where the speaker is off on a tangent while the audience patiently—at least at the outset—waits for the important part of the presentation to begin.

Don't let that be you. For the average public speaker, if you want to be effective, remember to have a plan, maintain a good pace, and stay focused.

LAW #19: From the start of your presentation to the end, stay focused on the task at hand; a momentary lapse can derail a great presentation.

A.20: OFFENSIVE LANGUAGE

D o public speakers want to offend their listeners? Presumably not. Have we witnessed this happen? Likely more times than we care to recall. There are four areas of offensive language that I will highlight and that I suggest you avoid.

First, there is sexist language. A few years back at one of our ELO Forums we had a great speaker, a fellow in his mid 60s. There was, however, one noticeable shortcoming in his presentation. It sounded like fingernails on a chalkboard every time. He constantly referred to "businessmen," "us guys," his "guy buddies" and his "sporting pals." It sounded like he was talking to a men's locker room after hockey practice. What made this issue even more glaring was that his key executives were women in their 40s/ early 50s. Despite that, he sounded so out of touch. Sure enough, we got blow back after the event. His language should have been more inclusive and he could have used examples that would be familiar to more audience members. Unfortunately, we are not at the point where sexist language has been eradicated from the public speaking landscape. Sexism is, however, not the only form of offensive language.

A second form of offensive language relates to race and ethnicity. Public speakers should avoid any form of racial stereotyping. It happens often enough that it needs to be addressed. Having worked with many speakers over a long time, I believe the challenge generally is not that people are trying to be intentionally disrespectful, marginalizing or exclusive. I think in most cases it is a matter of not working to correct old habits, picked up in a different generation, and failing to deliberately appreciate the nature of what might be offensive today. Of course, there are much bigger societal issues such as "systemic racism" and the nature of subtle biases in collective behavior which are relevant. (In this book I can simply identify the challenge; it's far beyond the scope of this book to delve into a discussion of the issue). Of course, this law regarding offensive language is related to some of the other laws, such as how to connect with an audience (Law #11) and the need to do one's homework (Law #9). Connecting with an audience is hard to do if you are turning them off. You won't only alienate the people who are the direct subject of your remarks, but also the other people in the audience who don't appreciate a person alienating others.

When attempting humor in today's world, the safest approach is simply to stay away from humor that is based on race or ethnicity. When speaking in public, it is important to recognize how groups wish to be self-described, and be careful to speak respectfully of other groups in one's society. As mentioned elsewhere in this book, an approach of being belittling or demeaning to others is not good generally, and clearly not acceptable as a public speaker (Law # 27). There are many other avenues for humor; as mentioned in Law #15, you should poke fun at yourself. I do. I have lots of material to work with.

A third form of offensive language is swearing. The *Oxford English Dictionary* indicates that there are about 600,000 words in the English language, and this count is growing steadily. There is no shortage of material to work with. Of this great number, there are words that are generally regarded as profane, although that varies among English speaking countries. The best rule of thumb would be to avoid using any profanity from the platform. If you are in any doubt as to what is appropriate, ask the event organizers. Why bother raising this issue? Every once in a while, you do get speakers throwing "f bombs" from the podium. In some cases, this might just be their normal speech pattern, or perhaps they think profanity works as an effective exclamation point. However, when you curse on the platform, I think that the conclusion of most listeners is that you don't have enough of a vocabulary to express yourself effectively, with class and clarity. Many people swear in many situations; save it for when you are driving. This principle may seem like a double standard to some. At the same time, though, we don't see our political and business leaders swearing on the evening news.

The fourth area of offensive language relates to religious figures or concepts. Modern audiences are sensitive to many forms of offense, but because the history and culture of Western society is so steeped in Christianity, certain jokes and offensive slang have become the norm, and are part of the general lexicon. As a consequence, saying, "Oh, my God!" from the platform may seem classless, but it is not generally considered to be offensive. More specific swear words, such as to say, "Jesus Christ!" or "for Christ's sake," are, however, offensive to adherents of Christianity. Yes, many Hollywood movies and TV shows use those phrases as acceptable invectives but that does not mean that they are inoffensive or acceptable. Insulting any religious, ethnic, or cultural group is unacceptable on the podium. Yet, offending those who don't believe in taking the name of Jesus Christ in vain is seen as acceptable. I suggest that the above guidelines of not deploying offensive language applies to Christian beliefs. Just as you shouldn't make anti-Semitic or Islamophobic remarks, I would suggest not making remarks that would offend Christians.

Ultimately, the way to eliminate a person's use of offensive language is to go to the root of an individual's character. I think that the best approach to avoiding offensive language, if that is a problem, is to first change who you are, rather than how you speak. If you change who you are, and you are a thoughtful, articulate, and dignified person, then you simply bring that to the podium. If, one the other hand, offensive language is part of who you are and how you normally act, it takes extra effort to be on a podium and remember not to speak the way you normally would. I often meet speakers who are foul-mouthed and then need to turn on a switch as they walk to the podium to be careful about what they say. Be forewarned: it will come out somewhere, sooner or later(See Law #21).

LAW #20: There is nothing to be gained by using offensive language, whether it be sexist, racist, vulgar, or antireligious. Such language will only detract from your professionalism and your message.

A.21: THE MOST DANGEROUS 15 SECONDS

You can blow it all in only 15 seconds. You have prepared meticulously for your presentation. You have done your research. You have practiced. The content is great. Your presentation slides are even better. You have a willing audience. They are looking forward to what you have to say. You have practiced your entire speech, from start to finish. From the second you get to the podium to the second you get off, everything is all thought through—no word or hair is out of place.

Well, not quite. There is the brief interlude between getting to the podium and starting your presentation. These are the most dangerous 15 seconds of any presentation. This is when people start to ad-lib, go off script, think that they will slip in something funny, make an off-the-cuff remark, or try a quip. This is a very bad, high-risk idea.

I was at a national conference of about 600 businesspeople in Canada, and we were about to hear from a senior partner at the head office of one of country's largest accounting firms. He was the opening speaker. He was white, in his late 50s, with a shirt that looked better forty pounds ago. He came bounding on to the platform just like he had been instructed to by a consulting firm to show energy. He had a self-confident, nearly arrogant smile, with too many teeth. He conveyed, "I'm an expert and about to fill you in." Then he made what turned out to be the biggest blunder of the entire conference.

Let me provide some context first. The Prime Minister of Canada at the time, Justin Trudeau, apparently had some youthful indiscretions. Of course, once one is in the public eye, one's critics and opposing political parties will be working diligently to dig up past misdeeds. They succeeded.

Part of Justin Trudeau's preparation to lead the country was being a high school teacher. Apparently, one year the school had a dress-up party, and Trudeau decided to dress up in "blackface" (in other words, painting his face black to portray a black person). At the time, Trudeau apparently had no problem with this, and in fact had an ample supply of black makeup as he apparently used it on more than one occasion. It was only when a photo of Trudeau was produced years later, showing him in blackface and proving difficult to deny, that he realized the error of his ways and apologized profusely and continuously.

He was presumably sorry for the act itself, but even more sorry he got caught. This was a major kerfuffle in the media and even made headlines around the world. After suitable contrition and a commitment to better behavior in the future, it was eventually filed away to be trotted out when the next election campaign started. The media was ready to move on to the next day's main issues. To be clear, however, the notion of a white person dressing up in blackface was, of course, disrespectful, racist, and completely inappropriate. We all agreed on this point.

Back to the conference. This speaker came bounding up on the stage and got settled at the podium. Then, the first thing he said was, "Ha ha, at least I'm not dressed up in blackface for this presentation!" He had a smile on his face that became increasingly uneven as the room fell deathly silent. He waited for the laughter—and quickly realized it wasn't coming.

He had put his foot, his leg, and both arms in his mouth. He mocked an important issue. I remember settling into my chair, looking forward to hearing him, the first speaker. Then, when he made that remark, I thought to myself, "whaaat did he just say? Did he just say what I thought I heard?" At these moments, you tend to look to people beside you as if to confirm, "Did you just hear what I thought I did?" He made this comment prior to saying anything else, before establishing rapport with the audience, and before demonstrating any credibility. For the rest of the presentation, I couldn't get the impact of that remark out of my mind.

The intent of him speaking at the conference was presumably to represent his firm well, to demonstrate his own personal expertise, and to try to get business for the firm. He struck out on all three. In fact, his presentation backfired. You would intentionally not use someone like him. Over the coffee breaks and at lunch people were chatting about his remark.

Lo and behold, at the conclusion of the conference, the organizer announced that our opening speaker wants to make a cameo at the podium. Up he came awkwardly, due to the size of his tail between his legs, a smile turned to somberness, to apologize for his insensitive remark. He was in a difficult spot. To not come up would have left the issue hanging, but to come up also reminded everyone of his remark. Also, we didn't know if this was genuine—you said it, it slipped out, so you have revealed what you actually think. Now, you are simply being contrite because you realized the impact to your firm and the event organizer.

But why did this happen? He failed to show discipline in the first 15 seconds. He had an actual introduction to this talk—but this was the pre-talk 15 seconds. He should have had the discipline to stick with his presentation. His mistake, possibly hubris induced, is made frequently. During those first few seconds people say the worst things. Don't be one of them.

LAW #21: Beware of the first and most dangerous 15 seconds. Your presentation starts from the moment your name is called.

A.22: THE NEXT MOST DANGEROUS 15 SECONDS

Second only to the first 15 seconds, I have seen more good work undone in the last seconds of a presentation than at any other time. As with the introduction, the same perils apply. Don't fall into the trap of going off-script. End authoritatively and get off the platform.

Simply wrap up an obvious final point, look at the audience, and say "thank you." Perhaps wait briefly for applause, as appropriate. Then, get off the podium.

This shows confidence. You've done your job, you did it well, and it's time to wrap it up. A strong finish should have a punchy example and maybe a great quote to wrap it up, but regardless, with a well-organized talk, your audience should be able to tell when you are finished. You have gone through to your last point, so then you sum it all up and say, "I'd like to leave you with this final thought." Think of it as ending with an exclamation point.

One of the common ways to have a great ending to your presentation is to move from the general and theoretical to the personal. I have found that too many people want to stay in the realm of the theoretical; this is not impactful. Let's say the presentation was about the public speaking laws of success. I might talk about key principles throughout the presentation, but at the end I would focus on you. Now that you have heard about these key principles and the difference they can make in the personal and professional aspects of your life, what are you going to do about it? Let me suggest that before you leave this ballroom that you commit to finding and securing one speaking opportunity within the next 30 days. Practice is your pathway to success.

By contrast, don't finish a presentation with a whimper. One of the worst things you can do is, instead of finishing strong, just keep talking in circles, and then say something like, "Well, I guess that's it." It's like the difference between watching a bad or good movie. A bad one feels like it is going nowhere and then it simply ends. A good movie always reaches a crescendo at the end, the plot is solved, and there is a satisfying denouement. Just as races are often won just before the finish line, your presentation can live or die by its conclusion.

This approach is not only important when you are at the podium in front of a large crowd, but also in different contexts such as a business boardroom. I have seen, for example, a great sales presentation undermined in the last 15 seconds. Let's say you are doing a presentation to pitch your firm's consulting services. As part of the presentation, you convey to the prospective client that your firm is doing well. You do a good job with this presentation and it is generally well-received. The prospective client taking comfort in the fact that you are a busy and desirable consulting firm.

You finish the presentation. The tension has dissipated. You have a palpable sense of relief, and instinctively, you let your guard down. As you walk out of the board room and almost to the elevator lobby, one listener asks, "Hey, so how many files do you have on the go right now?" You are caught a bit off guard, and because you have created some connection during your presentation, you think you can confide in the person. You say, "Actually, we're not that busy right now and could really use this assignment." Ouch. You have just revealed your hand. The bravado, the confidence you displayed for an hour has, with one unwise comment, instantly dissipated.

I have seen many deals and opportunities go sideways in the last 15 seconds of a presentation or immediately thereafter. Don't let that be you. As soon as the presentation is done, wrap up politely and get out of the room. Your presentation isn't over until you are out of the building.

> **LAW #22:** Be very careful about the last 15 seconds of your presentation. You can undo all the good work you have done for an hour. Remember: when you're done, get off the stage and out of the building.

B—KEY PRINCIPLES

B.23: FEEDBACK FROM YOURSELF & OTHERS

The keynote speaker for this event had knocked it out of the park. The attendees loved the presentation. He told several engaging stories, and people were enthralled. The response forms confirmed my own impression of him, and he turned out to be one of our most highly ranked ELO speakers over the past 15 years. You'd think this would mean that everyone was happy—but this wasn't the case. I spoke to one of the attendees a few days later, and while we were talking I asked him, "Hey, so what did you think of our keynote?" I thought I would rekindle some good memories.

"Well, he told a lot of stories," this attendee replied dismissively. "I wasn't too impressed." I was taken aback. Upon reflection, I concluded that this comment revealed more about this person than the speaker. This attendee is an occasional public speaker who does a decent job without flash or pomp, and rarely tells a story. The reality was that, yes, the evening keynote speaker had told a number of stories—and he nailed it.

This attendee didn't get it, though. He couldn't get outside his own perspective to provide a balanced assessment of the presentation. While the speaker did an outstanding job, this person was not impressed for reasons that had little to do with the speaker's actual skill. So, was this worthwhile feedback? To assess feedback you receive, you need to be able to do some detached self-reflection as a starting point, and then solicit and filter feedback from outside yourself.

First, how can we do appropriate self-reflection? Donald Schon, author of *The Reflective Practitioner* (1983), highlighted in his book the fact that there is a difference between the knowledge that we acquire through formal education, and the knowledge that we acquire while engaged in our work. Schon examined various professions. He identified that the ability to reflect meaningfully on one's own experience was an important and distinct skill. In other words, thinking through one's own performance, or "reflection in action," in an objective, somewhat detached manner, is essential to success. The successful person thinks, "I have just completed a task. What did I learn? Did it confirm certain things I knew?" The outcome of this process is that a person can increase their skill level over time by being an efficient learner. Schon realized that many people do not reflect meaningfully on their own experiences and their interactions with others, both within their professions and elsewhere.

A related concept is "emotional intelligence," which provides a groundwork for understanding the importance of self-awareness. David Goleman, author of *Emotional Intelligence*, was a key figure in the popularization of this idea. Goleman was writing with respect to leaders, but I would say the same principle applies to effective public speakers. In his book, he concluded that "the most effective leaders all have a high degree of emotional intelligence." Fortunately, these skills can be learned. One component of emotional intelligence is "self-awareness." This includes the ability to recognize and understand your own moods, emotions, and drives, as well as their effects on others. A realistic self-assessment is a hallmark of emotional intelligence. Careful self-reflection is a great way to keep improving in every area of life, and the same goes for public speaking. As you engage in public speaking in various contexts, you need to be able to reflect meaningfully on each experience. Regardless of how often you speak in public, you should use the principles of emotional intelligence to get better every time. How could you do that? There are some very simple ways.

First, if your event is recorded, take a look at the recording. Your first reaction will be: "Do I really walk like that? Do I really stand like that? Is that really what my voice sounds like? Do I really look that overweight?" OK, maybe that last one is just me. In any event, back to you. Sadly, the answer is yes, that recording is indeed how you appear to other people. When you watch the recording, you will pick up many details that you would not have been aware of while speaking—things like the pace of your speaking voice, your hand gestures, the number of filler words that you use, and so on.

Second, ask the organizer for good feedback. If an organizer does events regularly, then that organizer will have a very good idea as to how to put you in the context of many other speakers. Sometimes, though, the organizer will be reluctant to give you candid feedback, because that will make them the bearer of bad or uncomfortable news. Most people do not appreciate or want honest feedback—thus it is rarely given. Make sure the organizer knows you really want to hear how you did, flaws and all.

Thirdly, you can ask for a summary of the collective audience feedback, if available. At ELO Forums, attendees fill out response forms. I have found that these response forms are very helpful for a number of reasons. When you get hundreds of responses it balances out the extremes, so you get a good cross section of the overall opinion. Although we don't offer anonymous response forms, most people are quite honest in their assessments, as they don't personally know the presenters. I have found that getting feedback from the entire audience generally produces a consensus opinion of 80–90%, with 5–10% at each extreme. If you take advantage of this resource, you will have an advantage over the vast majority of speakers.

Fourth, you may also get random audience feedback, at the event or shortly thereafter. Make sure you exercise some discretion in this situation. An attendee may come up to you and praises your presentation profusely, but if you take it as confirmation of a job well done without looking for additional context, you might not get the full picture. Out of the entire audience, that might have been the one person who wanted to work at your company. Individual feedback, without reference to other sources, may be misleading.

While the above four methods of feedback are useful, you still need to take a balanced approach of filtering feedback and separating the wheat from the chaff. You may be subject to criticisms that betray a lack of knowledge or experience. "I wish you would have spoken longer, covered this topic, taken more questions," someone might say. However, you had time constraints, the topic was intentionally narrowed, and there was a limit on how many questions you could answer. I have found that some forms of feedback are not worthwhile (i.e., some people have a particular axe to grind). What to do?

Make sure you're getting feedback from a competent and trusted source: someone who knows how to do public speaking, and who has your best interests in mind. I have many long-time advisors who have contributed to ELO and I always do a debrief with them after our Forums. For example, one of my best sources of feedback is an experienced and very successful entrepreneur, now in his late 70s. He is a great supporter of the ELO Forum we host in his city and he has the success of myself and the event at the forefront of his mind. His insightful comments are like gold.

LAW #23: The art of self-reflection and soliciting and filtering feedback are critical components of the ongoing process of continuing to improve as a public speaker.

B.24: PLAY TO YOUR STRENGTHS

"**I** call B.S.!" This phrase is often heard around the campfire, in the backyard, and by the barbecue. In polite company with more expensive meals, people may not say it—but they'll be thinking it all the same!

Sometimes, for a speaker, the lure of the platform overshadows one's better judgment. That's unfortunate. One of the fastest ways to lose credibility is to speak on a topic you don't know much about. Make sure that, whatever you do, you only speak on topics you know something about, either through personal experience or thorough study. Don't try to bluff your way through any topic. You might do that while chatting with your buddies in a private conversation, where your insights will soon disappear with the afternoon sun, but don't do it from the podium. While no one is likely to stand up and call you out, the audience will all realize it as you are speaking. Confident and competent people are very good at sticking to subjects they know well.

There are other instances where people step outside their comfort zone, when it's not a matter of professional expertise, but rather familiarity with the subject matter to be discussed. I witnessed a classic example of a person getting outside an area of knowledge a few years ago. Across North America, there are events called "prayer breakfasts." The ostensible purpose is for the religious community of a particular city to get together and pray for their political leaders. We all agree that they could use all the help that they can get. It is meant to be done in a non-partisan manner. These events started in Seattle, WA in the 1950s, and now are held throughout the Western world. The events have a Christian foundation and typically feature speakers who are aware of the Bible. They work hard to include local politicians, business leaders and community organizers, and thus the flavor is a bit broader than a hardcore flock of the faithful.

In one city, the prayer breakfast is attended by over 1,000 souls. The higher-profile politicians are then assigned various tasks in descending order of spiritual import to lure them onto the podium. The politicians do things such as reading from the Bible (they make sure it's not upside down), providing some opening remarks, or doing a prayer. One year, there was a big city mayor was tapped to do the opening prayer.

He started by greeting everyone, from the religious to the irreligious, and established his spiritual chops by confirming like Kris Kristofferson in "Sunday Morning Coming Down" that he once heard the bells of a church in session. He began to pray: "O Lord... Our Father, oh Mother Earth, Supreme Being, Great Spirit in the Norman Greenbaum Sky, Wind, Earth and Fire, or whatever you are, if you are up there, or down here, or somewhere in between, and whatever we imagine you to be, and it's all good anyway, please bless this event and the food we are about to eat, and bless the hands that have made it, the farmers who grew it, the trucks that brought it, the people who did the oil changes, and anyone else I missed, we ask these things in your name, your son and the rest of the family. Amen." I could barely contain myself from bursting out in laughter. I thought I just witnessed a parody on Saturday Night Live. The mayor was an island of spiritual awkwardness in a sea of holiness. The best course of action would have been not to speak. Or he could have gone with a safe bet, like the Lord's Prayer. The desire to speak in front of a crowd overshadowed his better judgment.

Another example comes to mind, not farcical but rooted in misjudgment. I had lined up a speaker with an amazing pedigree. He had run a large global organization, with thousands of employees, and billions in revenue. The company was well-known throughout the globe. I wanted him to simply tell his personal and business journey. What a fascinating story! How do you get to the top of this type of behemoth? How do you manage an organization of this size? Can you really make a difference? We were going to find out. Actually, we weren't. He had decided instead to provide an economic analysis of the current global situation. He was an erudite and learned individual. His instinct was not to focus on himself and his own experiences, and share stories (probably a bit light and fluffy), but rather deliver something of substance. That he did. He sounded like he was reading *The Economist*. The net result was that it was a lackluster presentation and not well-received. His mistake was that he didn't play to his strengths. He didn't realize what the attendees wanted to hear from him: they didn't want an economic analysis. They wanted his story. I think the reason he didn't deliver is because he thought it was too trivial.

Another example of the importance of playing to your strengths is the speaker who has had success in one endeavor and is now trying to leverage that expertise to a broader sphere. A classic case is that of the professional athlete. Some athletes are on the speakers' circuit, and they effectively tell their story. It's good for what it is. They talk about some familiar names, give the behind-the-scenes information, and recall the winning locker room. It's interesting, and we as the audience can learn a bit (see Law #43). That's an excellent evening keynote, but can you take what you learned in sports, and then build an entire presentation, book, and career out of your sports experiences? Generally, no, you cannot. An example is a training session I was part of that was led by a former athlete. He was a very accomplished individual, and was at the top of his field in the world. His applications of lessons to business were razor thin, but that wasn't all. He had also discovered his own path to find meaning in life, and he insisted on sharing it. He shared all his views on how faith is a supernatural ability to thrive in chaos and doubt, and how to get providence on your side. He was an erstwhile "new age guru lite." In truth, he was entirely out of his element. You can't teach a turkey to fly.

Be aware of your strengths and play to them. Think through your particular strengths. What can you deliver uniquely, that the audience would be interested in? Work that into your examples in your presentation. It's not what you want to say, it's what the audience wants to hear.

LAW #24: Always play to your strengths and leverage your expertise; if you speak from a foundation of knowledge, that will separate you from the rest.

B.25: EMBELLISHMENT

Years ago, my good friend Malcolm Gladwell and I spoke together at a conference for a combined fee of $100,000. We both performed admirably well and collectively spoke before over 1,000 attendees! I hope you are impressed. Well, actually, there are a few more details. Malcolm did the keynote for $100,000. I was way down on the undercard, and was paid what I was worth at the time—zero. I consider him a good friend, having shaken his limp hand once, but I suspect my characterization of our relationship is not reciprocated. We both spoke well, Malcolm to over 1,000 people and me to under 1,000 people.

I give this example to show how easily speakers, and people generally, can distort reality. The best approach: simply tell the truth. This becomes particularly relevant in terms of how speakers describe themselves and their accomplishments to build their credibility. Always remember that you should be introduced as the person you are, not the one you wish you were.

Generally speaking, the more you have done, the less you need to say. Most professional speakers like to keep their introductions brief, and in fact, if the introduction is already in the conference material, they don't need it read out at all. They know they will be judged on their presentation. Nevertheless, for most speakers a brief introduction is needed to establish some credibility and to answer the question, "Why are these people going to listen to me?"

If you embellish your resume and people catch on to it, you will lose credibility. Of course, if you go into politics you will have professional and motivated fact-checkers to contend with, as well. Speakers and others commonly misrepresent their background. For example, "Mr. X is a graduate of Smallville Junior State College, and is a graduate of the

Harvard Business School." We as the audience are meant to be impressed that while, through no choice and plain circumstances, this individual was bound to go to the local college because it was within walking distance, he managed to hit the big leagues and graduated from the Harvard Business School. That would be an impressive feat. But did it happen that way?

Well, no, not quite. Harvard has made monetizing its brand into an art form. Harvard has an Owner/President Management (OPM) Program offered for a series of three week stints over three years, weighing in at a hefty US$120,000 price tag. This is an open enrollment program. You need to meet some basic criteria, such as a business track record, but essentially a check and a pulse are the two most important qualifications. By paying the money and completing the program, you can become part of the distinguished global network of Harvard Business School alumni. Are you, however, a graduate of the Harvard Business School? That's a stretch. It would be better to introduce yourself as having completed a continuing education/open enrollment program at Harvard.

Tyra Banks, the businesswoman and supermodel, is a high-profile example of this situation. In 2012, Banks was exposed as having embellished her supposed Harvard credentials. Banks previously completed the aforementioned OPM program. Participants in the program are called "clients," not "students," as they do not have to take a GMAT to enroll. It's not part of the university's top-ranked MBA program, and the alumni of the OPM program are not granted a degree. As the website Jezebel. com pointed out at the time, attending the OPM program and calling it "going to Harvard Business School" is a little like enrolling in a pottery night class and saying you are "going to art school."

Another example along the same lines is people claiming affiliation with the University of Oxford. Misrepresentations are easy since Oxford is, of course, both an academic institution and a city. A further complication is that the University of Oxford is composed of 38 colleges and six "permanent private halls." As a result of this decentralized structure, the "Oxford brand" is more difficult to monitor. So, what does it mean if you hear of an "Oxford Summer Program" or "Smallville State College Oxford Program"?

I asked this question of the dean of a U.S. business school who said they had an Oxford summer program, and that their students studied at the University of Oxford. In answer to my questions, I learned that their Oxford program consisted of renting rooms at one of the colleges of Oxford with which it had no institutional arrangement. It simply rented space in the summer. The instructors were all from the small state college, and traveled to Oxford to teach—so they weren't Oxford instructors. Nevertheless, the college was running an "Oxford Summer Program," and all their instructors were now termed "Oxford instructors." The bottom line is that anyone could rent any room in Oxford and claim to be a graduate of an Oxford Institute.

If you make this kind of claim, you also need to be careful what you say. For example, if someone represents to be a "professor" at Oxford, that is a big claim. At Oxford, very few instructors become full professors or are permitted to refer to themselves as professors. There are many very distinguished teachers who are termed "lecturers" or "readers." There are many cases where people's credibility has been questioned and undermined by embellishment when they have referred to themselves as an "Oxford Professor." Regrettably, this has included some high-profile speakers. By contrast, in the North American context, it is more common to toss around the term "professor" in a very generic manner. Don't wait for someone to do fact-checking to phrase your resume correctly.

Another common form of embellishment surrounds the reference to a PhD. There are, for example, cases when someone uses the title of "Dr." despite not actually having a PhD. Many people who ask to be addressed as "Dr." are regularly exposed as never actually having had a doctorate. You may be aghast. Me too. This is quite a major embellishment, as a PhD is typically a four-year, full time endeavour. Even if you have "a doctorate from the school of hard knocks," if you don't have a PhD, then don't represent yourself as having one. I know that this sounds quite basic, but it needs to be clear. A milder form of embellishment is to stretch the credibility that a PhD offers. These days with the proliferation of educational institutions a PhD confers only a qualified credibility. We need to know more. Why? In an all too typical case, one contact got his PhD from an online institute above a fried chicken joint in a strip mall, and has been loudly proclaiming himself to be "Dr. So-and-so" ever since. Don't let your self-promotion outstrip your genuine academic credentials.

A final example of embellishment relates to TED talks. TED has become one of the world's best-known conferences—and for good reason, as many of the presenters deliver exceptional "set pieces." The better-known presentations have been viewed tens of millions of times on YouTube. There is a high degree of status associated with a TED Talk delivered at a TED Conference. However, a source of controversy and confusion is the fact that TED licenses its brand, which dilutes its credibility significantly. So, anyone—literally anyone—can hold a "TEDx event" that is loosely affiliated with, but not reviewed or sanctioned by, TED. Beware of claiming that you delivered a "TED Talk" by speaking at one tiny TEDx event hosted by the University of the Fertile Valley. Only the people you are not trying to impress will be.

In short, maintain the integrity of your bio. Remember that many people can read between the lines and see through your embellishments. You don't want to lose your credibility before you open your mouth.

LAW #25: Present yourself as who you are, not who you wish you were. It's much better to understate your credentials and over-deliver on your presentation than the other way around.

B.26: DRUNKS, PROSTITUTES & BULLS

The audience member was plastered, inebriated, just plain drunk—but he was still standing (barely). I had been invited to do a presentation during a happy hour segment, starting at around 5:30 p.m. after happy hour had been going on a while. The event was being held on the second floor of a small downtown building with a buzzing crowd of about 50–60 people. The drinks were set up, unmonitored, on a small table in one corner of the floor; music was blaring in the background. The event coordinators were to get people to stop their chatter and direct attention to the corner of the room, where I would be doing my thing.

I was ready to get going. The emcee got most people's attention, and I launched into my talk. A few minutes into my presentation a fellow standing at the front of the crowd, with a drink in his hand, belted out a semi-coherent question. At first, I couldn't quite make out what he was asking, and I wanted to take him seriously, so I guessed at what the question meant and tried to give an answer. I thought that might placate him. I was wrong.

I tried to continue with my talk, only for him to half-shout another question. This one was hard to understand, let alone to answer. I tried to acknowledge the attempt and keep moving on, but I quickly realized that he was quite inebriated, and that placating him was not going to work. I shortened my presentation and kept going through it while maintaining a rearguard action to fend off his comments.

In the end, I finished my presentation, and probably scored a few points for dealing with the rabble-rouser calmly and diplomatically. It was on the verge of going sideways, but ultimately it could be controlled. Of course, I was not impressed with the organizers of the event who should have dealt with the situation, but the audience was watching me and judging how I dealt with it.

This is a valuable lesson. When speaking in public, remember in the back of your mind that you need to be ready for anything. This type of disruption is not uncommon, if you speak long enough and in a sufficient variety of venues. I have experienced this a couple of other times, mostly at weddings with open bars. In one instance, while the bride was making her speech, you could hear someone add colorful commentary—quite loudly—at regular intervals. It soon became clear that the garbled voice was from an inebriated guest. The bride did the right thing by continuing with her address. The situation was not ideal, but it was tolerable. If you are in the same situation, you should continue as long as it is not too distracting. If it gets too extreme, then graciously stop your presentation and ask to speak to the organizer to have it dealt with.

The issue of hecklers is nothing new. Take, for example, John Wesley, the founding father of Methodism in 18th century England. It is estimated that he rode 250,000 miles and preached more than 30,000 sermons in his lifetime. He encountered his fair of challenges while preaching.

One of his biographers, Stephen Tomkins, notes in *John Wesley: A Biography* that while Wesley was preaching, "two singers were paid to interrupt his sermon by performing a ballad." In another case, "in Deptford, [England], a group of prostitutes was procured to disturb the gathering." This certainly seems like a novel and seldom-used approach. In other instances, "more than once, Wesley came home to find angry crowds lying in wait." Lastly, a personal favorite of mine is when "[in Bristol, Wesley] was attacked by a hired gang who tried to drive a bull at them." In sum, many great speakers have faced challenges while in the midst of their presentations.

Would it have been useful for me to get angry with someone who has had a few too many? No, likely it would have made things worse and people would have been focused on my reaction rather than the source of the disruption. Be calm and carry on, as best you can.

LAW #26: Remember to keep your composure. People will judge you by your actions as much as by your words.

B.27: ABUSE OF THE PLATFORM

"The cupcake lady went over time, and I will, too!" This is what one of our speakers said about an earlier presenter on the program. Why make the snide remark? I have no idea, but I have witnessed many comments of this ilk.

In this particular situation, we had a full-day ELO Forum planned. There were a number of presenters, and we worked hard to keep everyone within the time constraints. One speaker, mentioned in a previous chapter, had started a chain of cupcake shops. Despite our previous instructions, she went slightly over time; however, she did a great job on her presentation.

The next speaker was a seasoned executive in his mid-50s, with a manufacturing corporation. He was a straight-shooting speaker. He knew the time constraints, and knew that we would not reduce his time due to other people going long. He simply wanted to lengthen his presentation because some one else went overtime on hers. He blurted out his comment. He didn't wait for an audience response, just kept on talking. He left a sour taste in people's mouths. "What a jerk," many people commented in their response forms. It took his likability factor way down.

I call this an "abuse of one's platform." This is a bigger issue than one rude presenter. Speakers abuse the privilege of being onstage. Perhaps they believe that because they can hurl some invective, insults and cynical remarks without any pushback, they are free to do so without any consequences. While you are onstage, you can say a lot of things, and short of the organizer running up to toss you off (which is likely in the imagination but not execution), no one will stop you. However, beware that you will have burned a bridge with your remarks, and the consequences offstage will be long-lasting.

I have seen this abuse of the platform happen regularly enough that I can clearly say it is a problem. I have organized conference in various cities, and not every location is as nice as the other. I have had speakers start off by saying, I'm glad to be in [Smallville], despite the lousy weather and the fact that there is nothing to do. Ha ha!" If you were recently in Paris, London, or New York, and now you are in Cleveland—find something nice to say about Cleveland.

In other cases, speakers insult and throw barbs at me, the conference organizer. There is a saying: "Don't bite the hand that feeds you." It's a cliché for a reason. I'm not quite sure why someone would lash out at their host. Do you show up at your friend's place for dinner and say, "It's about time you invited me over?" No, that would be rude. However, some speakers seem to think they can do exactly that.

On one occasion, I had a seasoned and quite successful businessperson who turned out to be an awful public speaker. For some reason, he spent the first few minutes of his presentation talking about me. This is in a room full of people who generally know me and come to my events regularly, so they are my supporters. Nevertheless, he said, "I know Rick wanted me to speak about XX, but I will be speaking about YY instead. I know Rick must be cringing right now and squirming in his seat, but I am going to discuss YY anyway." Besides the fact that he was a poor public speaker, it's hard to say what led to his approach. I guess, for many people, it's a way of trying to be funny—to have someone else be the butt of their jokes. You ridicule someone or some location. One thing that is certain, though, is that if you are negative from the platform, it will be magnified. You will be displaying a deep-seated cynicism. If your intent is to be funny, then find some other ways of integrating humor into your presentation.

Another variation of abuse of platform is using your speaking opportunity as a soapbox. In other words, now that you have a captive audience, you are going to perform a public rant or give your opinion on some topic of the day—not because anyone is interested, but because you can. Maybe you begin to rant about the nature of air travel. "There are so many lineups and delays, and it's so aggravating," you say. "Why can't it be simpler and more efficient?" And so it goes. Unless you were invited to speak on this topic, though—don't bother. Therapy might be more appropriate. Or, as a less expensive option, you can go to the Speaker's Corner in Hyde Park. Your soapbox will be waiting, an audience may not.

You have been entrusted with an opportunity to speak from the podium for a specified amount of time. You have been asked to speak on a certain topic. Any rude or cynical remarks are off-putting and unnecessary. Most organizers will not rush the stage and drag you off yelling and screaming, but when the event is over, you will not be invited back again or introduced to anybody—and the organizers won't provide a reference.

LAW #27: You will do yourself a great disservice if you abuse the platform you have been given; you will burn a bridge and ruin relationships.

B.28: SPEAKER'S HARA-KIRI

Hara-kiri. A form of sushi? No: hara-kiri is a Japanese term defined as the ritual suicide of a samurai by disembowelment with a sword, usually performed to avoid facing dishonor or death at the hands of adversaries.

What's that got to do with public speaking? People may commit a sort of metaphorical hara-kiri on the platform. In other words, speakers undermine the effectiveness of their own otherwise reasonably good presentation by making some specific act or faux pas. This can take various forms.

First, you may have made a false assumption related to the logistics of your presentation. This may not necessarily be a lack of preparation. Here's a befuddling example. I previously worked for a firm where we organized a workshop for about 75 business leaders and prospects. The concept was that we would have a lawyer, an accountant, and a financial planner all do 20-minute presentations, then follow up with a 30-minute group Q&A session. They were all covering different angles of the same general topic.

The accountant provided a great presentation. The financial planner did likewise. Lastly, our distinguished member of the legal profession got to the podium and started her presentation. The cover slide was fine. Then she got to her first content slide. She hesitated. She had just realized that it was the wrong presentation. Her assistant had changed the cover slide but not the substance of the PowerPoint slides.

She started to stammer out excuses. "Sorry, this is the wrong presentation. Oh, just hang on. Well, I can continue." The audience watched as she fumbled around to find the right presentation. She was doing her prep work in front of everyone.

There were a lot of things that episode conveyed. First of all, it was extremely disrespectful to the organizer, and more so to the audience, to be so careless and nonchalant. It wasted everyone's time. Further, such a presentation would not help in any business development endeavors—rather, this speaker's engagement actually backfired. It is hard to be inspired by the professional competence of a lawyer who can't even handle doing a presentation properly. Needless to say, she was never invited back again.

A second form of hara-kiri is to be too self-promotional. The degree to which you as a presenter are promoting yourself and your services should be sorted out with the organizer in advance of your presentation. Don't leave it to an unspoken understanding. In various business contexts, a speaker will be invited by a group to do a presentation. There is no reasonable fee or compensation, just the specter of securing clients for their services (products or consulting) and, if they have them, book sales. A common, basic misunderstanding is that some speakers will take on an opportunity knowing that they want to sell something to make it worthwhile, when the organizer is expecting them to focus on educating the audience. Another component of the equation is the expectation of the audience. If they have paid for the event, they will typically be expecting content rather than a sales pitch.

A speaker will suffer "speaker's hara-kiri" if they are too self-promotional, particularly when it is not expected. This approach will turn off the audience. If the speaker is continually interrupting the presentation to make self-promoting comments and to talk about their great products and company, it will be counterproductive.

Generally speaking, the best way to prevent this misstep is as follows. Be clear on the nature of the event and the sales expectations involved. Have the organizer or introducer highlight your company and its services, and your book, if you have one. Then, do a great presentation so that people want to engage with you. After your presentation, that's the time to connect with interested parties.

A different form of self-promotion is not related to sales but to bolstering one's ego. I once had a management school professor speak at one of my events. He was quite accomplished in his sphere and among his peers, but seemed to be frustrated by the limited esteem that was not due from his business contacts. As the session proceeded, he went on and on about how much money he made, and how much more it was than a "lowly professor" could typically bring in. Then he would talk about how many books he had written. The kicker, though, was the name dropping. He dropped virtually every name he could possibly think of, from political leaders past and present to the titans of business. Because he was speaking to a high level, executive education class, they saw through him like a window and it became almost comical. The speaker was so ensnared in his own insecurities that the listeners discounted his stories and, in fact, his overall credibility was undermined.

LAW #28: There is no more painful wound than the self-inflicted ones. Don't be your own worst enemy and commit speaker's hara-kiri.

B.29: MURPHY IS YOUR FRIEND

Murphy's Law: what can go wrong, may go wrong. We hadn't invited Murphy, but he certainly showed up that evening.

I had been looking forward to this event for months. My team of organizers had planned out all the details. It was going to be a dessert and coffee evening, as well as a book launch. People would show up and at the back of the room. We would serve coffee, tea, and drinks, and provide a delectable dessert buffet. The snacks would put everyone in a good mood. People would mingle around for about 30 minutes, and then we would start a more formal part of the program. I would open by talking about a book we were launching—a collection of interviews I had had with leading entrepreneurs. I was going to get up and make some remarks, and then the keynote speaker we had brought in would take over.

The venue was a beautiful setting. We had booked a local golf and country club. The ballroom had a sunroom, effectively highlighting the outstanding view of the golf course.

The day of the event came, and at first everything went as planned. After people had had their fill of dessert, we herded everyone to their seats. The bustle died down. I made my way to the podium. I remember the day like it was yesterday. I got up the podium, straightened my back, turned to face the crowd, and started to open my mouth. At that moment, all the power in the building went out. (One of my family members in attendance muttered, "Yes! There is a God!")

I was momentarily stunned. The lights were out, the sound system was shut off, and we could instantly tell that all power to the facility had been cut. As I quickly pondered next steps, a colleague from the Business School where I was teaching, came up and suggested that we cancel the event. My instant reaction was, "Are you crazy?!" I and many others had put in a lot of time and energy to have this event happen! I wasn't going to fold my tent so quickly. Our keynote speaker informed us that he wasn't going to do his hour-long presentation, typically accompanied with a slideshow, in the dark with no sound or technology.

Nevertheless, I decided on the spot that we must proceed as best we could. Someone from the crowd ran to the front and held a cellphone over the podium to provide me with light to read. Then others began using their phones for illumination, as well (bearing in mind that this was 2005, so not everyone had a phone, and the light was coming from the screens, not flashlights). The event staff began scurrying about the room and handing out candles. Soon enough, the room looked like a candlelight vigil. Looking out from the podium, it was a surreal sight. I managed to deliver a 15-minute overview of the event and concluded. The crowd gave a rousing round of applause.

The event turned out to be memorable, to the point where people still talk about it to this day. It also showed the necessity of quick thinking and taking action. The person who advised me to simply announce its cancellation was shown to be wrong: the show must go on. That night was the auspicious start of my organization, ELO, which has since held over 60 successful events across North America, Europe and Asia.

By the time we finally packed up, I was curious about how I could get home due to the power outage. I imagined that the suburbs must be in chaos, with streets clogged and intersections out of order, and the denizens fretting over thawing ice cream. I went to the parking lot and made my way to the exit of the golf and country club. There were high winds. A single massive fir tree had fallen on to a power line on the street right in front of the golf and country club. As I exited, I soon realized that in the entire suburb, only a single tree had fallen—and that was the one right in front of the club. Score one for Murphy.

I remember another noteworthy case in which Murphy reared his ugly head. I was involved in a high-tech venture start-up that was engaging in an early round of financing. I wanted to organize a venture presentation, but I also wanted to do something unique. I came up with the idea of a harbor cruise. The start-up was based in Vancouver, and there are several companies in that area which organize evening charters. I thought that a charter would be a great format, as we would have "captive" guests. Once they were on board and we were out in the harbor, everyone would be listening, and we would have time for ongoing chatter over the course of the three-hour harbor cruise. In addition, this activity was unique: many of the guests, including locals, had likely not been on an evening harbor cruise.

My organizing team and I had done our research and come up with a reputable company. We had selected a fine dinner menu. The boat was the right size for our group of 30. People slowly made their way to the marina and strolled up the gangplank, ready for an evening at sea. This was going to be fun. We were getting ready to start with dinner and the presentation, and then people could walk around and mingle for the rest of the evening. I hovered near the entrance to the back of the boat where people were entering to welcome them on board for the evening.

As I greeted the last straggler, I gave the agreed-upon signal to the captain that everyone had arrived. At first, I was focused on the guests, but after ten or fifteen minutes I thought it was odd that I hadn't heard the engines rumbling. I then noticed, out of the corner of my eye, that the hatch to the engine room below was open. That was odd. I discreetly moved to peer into the engine room below, only to overhear a string of expletives from the captain. I thought this was perhaps not a good sign. In fact, it was not a good situation, either. The engine wouldn't start. The crew worked on it for another 15 minutes before throwing up the white flag. This boat was not leaving the dock.

In light of my legal training, I instantly thought of the contractual breach and the damages flowing therefrom: a loss of face, a loss of credibility, etc. None of that helped in the moment, though. The only thing we as the organizers could do to salvage the evening was to proceed as normally as possible. The charter crew could still serve the meal, which they did. I, along with the founder of the company, went ahead with the presentation. Of course, it wasn't as nice as being on a harbor cruise, but in these situations, the show must go on.

We could still enjoy the meal. We could still do the presentation. We could still connect with people. And, in the end, we saved a bunch of money on the cruise as all fees from the charter company were waived. We also had a chance to show our character by demonstrating how we would proceed in less than ideal circumstances.

The chances of the power going out during your presentation are slim—I never had that happen before or since. The chances of a boat not being able to leave the harbor are also quite minimal. However, you need to be ready for any eventuality—and prepared to act decisively. The night of that power outage, my team and I had the gumption to keep going, and we haven't stopped since.

LAW #29: Make Murphy your friend. He won't show up often, but when he does, simply figure out how to work with him.

B.30: BRING YOUR "A-GAME"

Picture this: you are at a gathering of some sort. The last presentation is droning on and on. You are impatient to leave. You don't want to look rude by standing up and bolting for the door, but you do have things you need to do. They did say, after all, that it would end on the hour. Now, though, they are going over time.

You wait to make your move, looking for the nearest exit. *Can I make it look like I am going to the washroom? Not if I take my laptop with me*, you think. *Is it rude if I don't say goodbye to the people at my table? But if I do my plan will be revealed.* You decide to go for it. You wait for the speaker to turn to the other side of the room. You also want to leave before too many other people do, or your exit will become too noticeable.

We've all been in this situation. One particular instance stands out in my memory, though. Our ELO Forum was supposed to end at 9:45 p.m. sharp. After the keynote presentation was over, we planned to do a quick survey, as usual, to get feedback from attendees. This information gives us a good insight into what people think of the event, the speakers, etc. It's like gold to us, but on this particular evening, we weren't able to get nearly as many completed response forms as usual. The event ended with a whimper.

Our keynote speaker that night was very experienced, highly polished, and accustomed to addressing groups all over North America and throughout the world. In this instance, he was doing a good job with his keynote, but when he reached the requested 35-minute mark, he didn't stop. This speaker ended up going an extra 20 minutes: way overtime.

This extra time threw our evening session off kilter. People had already had a long day, and although the keynote was good, the way it dragged on left a bad taste in everyone's mouths. It made a poor finish of the entire event. Every time he looked to one side of the room a few brave souls on the other side bolted for the exits. The last 20 minutes were like a human sieve. We were able to get response forms from far fewer attendees than anticipated, and by the end of the night, there were a lot of empty seats.

What was most disconcerting to me, though, was that this exact same speaker did a phenomenal job in another location—and finished his presentation, the exact same presentation, on time. Yet, during that night's event, he went significantly over time. He seemed less focused, and his examples turned into long, rambling stories. I thought he might forget what city he as in.

In this case our speaker didn't bring his "A-Game." He might have packed too much into his schedule, he may have been jetlagged, or he may have been disinterested. In the end, the reason wasn't as important as the result.

It struck me that the same speaker was coming across very differently to two different audiences. In one city, his presentation was a home run; in the other, it fizzled out. I was reminded of stories about professional athletes and performers realizing that people are making it a priority to come and listen to, or be entertained by, the individual. It actually requires considerable discipline and commitment to bring your best—each and every day. It's human nature to get easily bored with the repetition. However, we must always have the audience in mind. This is just as true for any regular professional speaker as it is for athletes and musical performers. It may be the only time audience members ever see that person. The people who saw you at less than your best will assume that is your best.

You need to bring your A Game each and every time. If you can't deliver it, then you shouldn't get on the platform. Otherwise, you will have undermined your reputation.

LAW #30: Never commit beyond your ability to do your best at all times. You don't want to be defined by your worst performance, even by one person.

B.31: A TRUE STANDING OVATION

How can you get a standing ovation after a presentation? I mean a *real* standing ovation. There are, after all, at least two types of standing ovations. You've likely seen far more of the former than the latter.

The first type is the "contrived" standing ovation. Within that category there are a few different subtypes.

I have been at political gatherings where the audience is composed of those "drinking the Kool-Aid," so to speak, and then the rest of the crowd. The featured politician finishes up with final remarks, and then the sycophants spring to their feet like clapping seals, applauding so mightily it's like the roar of thunder. They are doing enough clapping for the rest of the crowd, and more importantly, for a photo from the right angle that can play on the news reel to show a tumultuous standing ovation.

The other type of "contrived" standing ovation is when you are at an event and a certain person is being honored. The person does their presentation and that person's supporters fill a handful of tables at the front of the room, making up perhaps less then 10% of all attendees. Their friend exits the stage, and they spring up on cue, clapping raucously—and not sitting down. They are making enough noise that the event can't really continue. There is then the tipping point where the rest of the crowd realizes that the event will not wrap up until this now-awkward moment passes, and they gradually stand up, due to some combination of expediency and sympathy, to help end the charade. It's also a good time for a stretch.

These two types of contrived standing ovations are not the ones I am talking about—although, on some level, they are better than nothing.

What makes a true standing ovation?

I have organized many events, with many speakers and attended many events, and I have experienced very few true standing ovations. However, I have experienced a handful of genuine ones, and they had some consistent features. First, the speaker gave transparent, moving and emotional remarks that resonated with the audience. Second, the speaker had great character traits, coming across as humble, often self-deprecating, and focused on the audience. Third, the substance of the speaker's remarks rang true with the audience. Lastly, the speaker's message was uplifting and inspiring. A standing ovation, in this case, is a form of saying "thank you."

One speaker who got a standing ovation at one of our ELO Forums was William (Bill) Pollard. At that time Bill was the Chair of Fairwyn Investment Company, a private investment firm. He was well-known in corporate circles, however, for another role. For a 25-year period, from 1977 to 2002, Bill participated in the leadership of The ServiceMaster Company and served not once but twice as its Chief Executive Officer. He also served as Chair of the Board of ServiceMaster from 1990 to April 2002 and was elected Chair Emeritus in 2002 when he retired from the Board. During his leadership of ServiceMaster, the company was recognized by *Fortune* magazine as the #1 service company among the Fortune 500, and was included as one of its most admired companies. During this period, ServiceMaster also was identified as a "star of the future" by *The Wall Street Journal* and recognized by the *Financial Times* as one of the most respected companies in the world.

When Bill was invited to speak at one of our ELO Forums, it soon became clear that he lived his values and that his integrity came from deep within his soul. He delivered a great presentation and he responded during the Q&A in an authentic and thoughtful manner. At the time of this presentation Bill was around 80, with a full head of gray hair, a grandfatherly demeanor, and the look of a wise sage. The whole time people were thinking, "Here is a fellow with endless accolades, and yet he is talking to us like a friend." When he finished speaking, I was in the process of getting out of my chair to make my way to the podium and thank him. Then, out of the corner of my eye, I saw the rest of the crowd springing up to give him a well-deserved standing ovation. Why? He had great content, outstanding character and a message of encouragement to other leaders, delivered by an elder statesman to young leaders.

Another time I witnessed a true standing ovation was when Peter Legge delivered a keynote presentation at one of our ELO Forums. I have mentioned Peter elsewhere in this book. Peter is one of North America's top public speakers for a reason, and on this particular occasion he gave his typical inspiring message. I think what put him over the top that day, though, was the way he shared openly about some of the projects he was working on. It struck me—and likely others in the audience—that he was being very transparent with things that were in process. He wasn't sure how they would turn out. He explained that he had put his heart and soul into a proposal and was desperately hoping it would turn out, but wasn't sure that it would. Many speakers will talk about something after the fact, when the outcome is clear and there is no risk of embarrassment. Not so for Peter. He laid it all out before us. People sensed he was taking a personal risk in sharing a dream that was still in the balance, and for that, like Bill, he received a standing ovation.

How can you achieve a standing ovation? It's not easy, and may never happen, but it is worth striving for. There need to be a few key elements. The content is important, but even more importantly, it needs to connect with people on an emotional level. It must ring true. The character of the speaker is vital. The audience must respect the speaker, and even admire them and what they stand for. The context must be right, due to the timing, the group, or the organization.

If you ever get a true standing ovation, know that you will have hit a grand slam in extra innings to win the game.

LAW #31: To receive a standing ovation is a rare, but possible, feat based on a combination of your presentation, the audience, the occasion and the timing.

B.32: PRATFALLS & PITFALLS

As you engage in public speaking, it is inevitable that you will experience your own pratfalls. You will also likely experience the various pitfalls of public speaking. No matter. You are not defined by pratfalls and pitfalls. Just keep moving on.

<u>Pratfalls</u>—If you speak often enough you will experience your own pratfalls. You will do something stupid that you wish you could take back. The problem is that once the mistake has been made, you are then doing damage control. Most pratfalls are not mean spirited, but things that might have been ad-libbed may cause offense, or deliberate actions on your part might have been misinterpreted. This is why, in politics, advisors are always sweating when their leader goes off script.

I have had my share of pratfalls. Despite our best intentions, all of us do stupid things sometimes. I have emceed at over a hundred events around the world, yet I still always need to remind myself to be careful. For example, at ELO forums, part of my role as emcee is to introduce and thank table hosts. Most of these table hosts are people I know relatively well. One year I was going through the introductions, bantering from the podium with the various table hosts as I introduced them. I then came to a couple who together owned a business and were table hosts. I had only recently gotten to know them. As they were introducing themselves one of them mentioned how long that they had been married. I responded that the guy was maybe a cradle robber and his wife must have been underage if they had been married that long. In the moment, that got a lot of laughs, and I couldn't see the looks on their faces from the podium where I stood. I didn't find out until the next year's ELO forum that they had felt like the butt of the joke, and they were mightily offended. Upon hearing their response, I sought them out to apologize and made amends.

<u>Pitfalls</u>—I have included in this list a number of pitfalls public speakers often face. Most can be anticipated and, hopefully, avoided.

<u>Attire</u>—Yes, it's important to look professional, but watch out for other clothing pitfalls you might not expect. One time, my company and I were in the middle of one of our conferences, and I couldn't figure out the source of that awful sound. I had been keeping in close contact with our sound crew to make sure all the minor details were taken care of, and all the speakers had been briefed on the type of microphones that were available.

Our speaker was all mic'd up and ready to go. She was a great speaker and quite energetic on the podium. She got up, did a short set of introductory remarks from the middle of the platform, and then started to walk across the stage. All of a sudden, we started to hear a loud crackle every few seconds. It was quite noticeable, so I hustled over to the sound crew. They checked the sound board and made adjustments, but nothing worked. Finally, we figured it out. The speaker was wearing very large, dangling earrings, and when she walked across the podium, the earrings would sway and hit the mic, making that loud noise. The bottom line: be careful what you wear, because unexpected things can trip you up.

<u>Microphone</u>—You will typically need to get "mic'd up" before your presentation. There are three microphone options: podium, lapel or headset. If you have the choice, select the one that works best for you. Make sure you check in with the sound desk well before you speak at an event. If your mic stops working during your presentation, which has happened to me, remain calm; a sound technician will typically come up and give you a new mic. While this is disruptive, it's better than an ongoing mic problem for your entire presentation.

<u>Sound Problems</u>—If you like to walk around while presenting, then make sure not to walk directly in front of the loudspeakers on the stage, or there may be a loud piercing sound! At one of ELO's events, we had large speakers sandwiching either side of the stage. One of our presenters kept walking close to the loudspeakers. The sound the speakers made definitely got people's attention—but it was incredibly disruptive. Always check

with your sound crew on a venue's special considerations before getting on stage.

Props—Generally, I don't advise using props. You should be able to deliver your message just by the power of your presentation. In particular, props in a business setting can look silly. For example, if you are explaining that you are going to "knock out" the competition and "go three rounds" with the champion competitor, you don't need to bring boxing gloves to the presentation, or to start shadowboxing. Yes, I have seen this happen.

Video—A video can be an effective part of a presentation, but generally you should show it at the beginning as part of the lead up, not during the presentation itself. If you show a video in the middle of a presentation, it can be very disruptive, especially when its momentum doesn't match the presentation. A poorly-timed video almost always ends your momentum, which is fragile and hard to recapture. Also, make sure it fits in well with your content. A good example of successfully using a video is when we at ELO had Mark Burnett speak at one of our events (see Law #13). He was very particular about showing an introductory reel right before he got up to speak. It was a very well done video, which highlighted a number of his shows and got people excited to hear him. Of course, a well-produced video can be expensive. I have had speakers with more limited resources use a video, and I typically advise against that, unless it is very good and it fits the presentation well.

Slideshows—Use presentation slides to enrich, not kill, your presentation. One great public speaker I have referred to elsewhere is Larry C. Farrell. He notes, "The amateurish use of [presentation] slides has destroyed untold numbers of otherwise decent presentations—yet it is the easiest thing in the world to correct." Here are Larry's two rules for dramatically improving your use of slideshows to support your message.

First, what should you put on the slides? Use a single photo or image covering one third to one half of the slide, plus a 'headline' across the top of the slide with 3 single line bullet points below—or, if it's more appropriate, use a powerful quote. That's the simple formula for success! Never, never, never fill a slide with a hundred words, or numbers, or multiple graphs and charts. Slides should not have exhaustive text. The objective is not to put your presentation on the screen. If your text is too small, it can't be read at the back of the room.

Second, how should you display the slides? Flash the slide on the screen to dramatically introduce the next topic or sub-topic, and then immediately explain the information on the slide by quickly describing the photo and literally reading the three bullet points of information. You can perhaps add an additional sentence or two to more fully describe each point, but do so quickly. Finally, draw the audience right back to yourself by facing them directly, more fully explaining the headline, and telling a story to more comprehensively describe each bullet point. Larry's approach: "I often prefer to just show the headline with the photo or graphic first, and then reveal each of the 4–5 bullet points one by one, giving a full description of each. This option really keeps you, the speaker, in control of the flow of information on the slide—and, of course, guides the audience's attention."

One other point regarding slideshows is one of my pet peeves. One classic rookie mistake is when, especially in a smaller meeting room, the presenter stands directly in front of the projector. Unwittingly, the presenter now has what looks like the mark of the beast on their forehead, or a very odd-looking tattoo. This situation can be very comical and it undermines a speaker's credibility.

> **LAW #32:** With experience, you will be able to minimize pratfalls and deal with the inevitable pitfalls of public speaking.

C—THE DIGITAL
ENVIRONMENT

C.33: THE SAME, YET DIFFERENT

Video conferencing technology has created the biggest dilution in company brand value since the dawn of the Internet. Why? Companies and their leaders are ill-equipped to use this new medium effectively. Better never to have tried, than to have tried and failed ignominiously. They seem to believe that since the sessions are being recorded from the comfort of their own home, that, well, they should look like they are being recorded from their own home. Many executives join video meetings slouched in their chair, drawling in a casual tone, with crayon stick figures pasted on the wall behind them. This behavior comes across as highly unprofessional.

At present, the most common video conferencing technology is Zoom, which has become the Kleenex of video conferencing. People will talk about Zooming, having a Zoom, sending a Zoom invitation. Another option is Microsoft Teams. In Section C I will speak about video conferencing generally, but the majority of my experience is with Zoom. Do people need help in this digital environment? Here's an example taken from a major bank's presentation I recently endured. The presenter was introduced, and then proceeded through his set of slides. He did not turn on his video. For a good 30 minutes, he explained his presentation with his voice as his only tool for connecting. The boredom of his audience was instantly magnified. The speaker should have known, or should have been instructed, to turn on his video and share his screen. The end result was that the bank's content didn't hit the mark; instead, the listener's conclusion was that a large national bank somehow, despite its hefty budget, didn't provide its speakers with the basic training to communicate effectively.

The digital environment can be a minefield of potential mishaps. While the digital environment is new and evolving, many of the public speaking laws of success still apply. What applies and what doesn't? That is the subject of this section. At ELO, we have successfully hosted many webinars and online conferences. I have interviewed many leaders and been interviewed in turn for many online events. With a firm grasp of the public speaking laws of success, applied in this new digital context, I have learned many valuable lessons.

Let me give one practical example of lessons learned in the marketplace. ELO has done over 60 in-person events in well-known cities such as Toronto, Singapore, Hong Kong, and Oxford. In 2020, in light of the COVID pandemic, we decided to move our events exclusively into the digital world. Many things changed. We cut down a one-day in-person event to a four-hour online experience. That seems to be the limit of time anyone is prepared to offer onscreen (and even that was too long for some people). We squeezed speakers into 30-minute slots, reduced from the usual 45 minutes. We adopted a Q&A format, since there needed to be a lot of back and forth—a set piece presentation is simply too boring watched through a screen. There are many additional items, which will be explained below.

Our focus was on making the events unique by emphasizing personal connections. We sold tickets in groups of 10. These forum groups met immediately before and after the event. This provided an opportunity for up to 10 people to meet in a Zoom chat. During the event, we made sure we have the chat function going, and encouraged people to introduce themselves. In addition to facilitating Q&A with the audience, we used the poll function as another way to get people engaged in the sessions. At the halfway point of the conference we had two 20-minute breakout sessions as another way for people to connect with others. The bottom line was that participants were able to connect with up to 20 other people. We also worked hard to have the sessions be engaging, so that it was not a passive experience like watching a TV show.

We have much to learn, but we did receive great feedback. We were able to provide great content, be engaging and facilitate interaction. For some people, the event was even better and more effective than the in-person experience would have been.

The digital environment presents an interesting balance with respect to public speaking. On the one hand, the ability to do public speaking well in the digital environment is rooted in the laws of success that we have highlighted throughout this book. On the other hand, the digital environment is a unique medium and some of the laws do not apply or they need to be modified. Video conferencing technology is a unique communication medium. It is not a matter of doing a presentation as if you were doing it in a board room. It's not the same platform.

The starting point is understanding the context of a presentation. In an online meeting, you are communicating with people who are somewhere else—whether at home, in the office, or on the beach—and you are trying to get and keep their attention. They are more easily distracted at the outset, and their thoughts will wander. Further, they can often exit the meeting with the click of a mouse.

You are also trying to connect with your audience. This is a challenge when you are not in person with them. The classic keynote is 45 minutes, usually taking place after dinner and combining some insights, good quotes, and well-told stories. These set pieces go over well when done properly, as the speaker interacts with the audience and laughter fills the room. That doesn't work online. In fact, I had one high-profile speaker who simply refused to do a presentation online. He realized that doing a presentation from his home office, to a dispersed online audience, in only 30 minutes, was going to cause a loss of magic.

LAW #33: To succeed as a presenter in the digital environment, one needs to adapt the fundamental public speaking laws of success for an online environment, because while many of the principles are the same, there are still many differences.

C.34: CONFERENCE PANELS & WEBINAR PRESENTATIONS

Being involved in a conference panel or as a sole webinar presenter online can make you feel like you are talking to yourself. With a live audience you can get a more tangible reaction, whereas over video calls you typically get very minimal feedback. There are some unique aspects of online events with which a speaker will need to contend.

One thing to bear in mind is the difference between doing a webinar presentation and delivering an online conference presentation. Many webinars are free and are done to promote a brand, make new contacts, and build up a company's influence. The audience expects that there will be some promotional aspect. An online conference is different. These are typically paid events. As a speaker, you will be expected to deliver more content and some clear takeaways so that there is some substantive value. Your promotional benefit will be through demonstrating your expertise. Any direct promotional aspect will be through the emcee's introduction and the conference organizer's promotion of your involvement. Here are a number of points to bear in mind when you are an online panelist or webinar presenter:

1. Time is value—the time of the panelists and host is valuable, and since they're allocating time to what they are doing, so should the listener. This is another reason why, if you are being interviewed or answering questions for the audience, responses should be in the 2–3 minute range. Long answers make audience members tune out and wait for the next question—if the answer is too long, they may tune out altogether!

2. The webinar is over after the host/interviewer finishes their concluding remarks and signs off. Be aware of how long you are

still on the screen. Once the host says goodbye, leave the meeting immediately.

3. Even if you have reviewed questions in advance with an event organizer, do not prepare a written response to read out. This will come across as stiff and lifeless. Instead, use notes or bullet points as a reference, but be sure to speak so that it appears spontaneous.

4. While you may be given a list of questions you will be asked, the host may integrate questions from the listening audience. It is much more compelling for the audience if they feel they are part of a live event, with at least some questions being addressed as they are posed, than it is if they are simply observing a static dialogue. People should feel they are part of the event, and there needs to be some engagement and evidence of that.

5. Be aware that there is typically a "hard stop" at the end of the allotted time. Keep your presentation short and to the point from beginning to end. People are busy, and they are more likely to watch a session if they know their time will be well spent. It's also easy for people to disconnect from a webinar, so it takes work to keep them. There is no social consequence for people to sign off early, and none of the awkwardness of slipping out of a room that comes with a live event.

6. Be aware that an event organizer will try to facilitate as much engagement as possible. Don't expect to present uninterrupted and then leave time for questions at the end, the way you would in a live setting. There should be constant interaction—otherwise, it's simply too boring. There should be interaction with the host as well as with the live audience. Your objective is not simply to get through your slide presentation. Your objective is to communicate and interact effectively.

7. One of the great things about webinars is that they can easily be recorded, and thus can be made available for viewing after the initial event. As a result, putting in the effort to do a webinar with excellence will have ongoing benefits.

8. The one error that I have seen frequently in the online webinar context is that presenters are too casual. A good level of casual is when a speaker works to be engaging and informal. However, when a speaker is too casual, it comes across as being unprofessional. I have seen several webinars begin with the moderator slouched in their chair or leaning back in an office recliner. It sometimes seems that people think that, because they are in the comfort of their own home, they therefore can relax. They don't recognize that they are presenting to an audience. Other speakers start by saying things like, "So, hey, yeah, like, welcome to this webinar, and, like, yo, it's going to be great." Instead, start off by sitting upright and ready with your carefully-constructed opening remarks.

9. Popular video conference technology is always trying to improve its function, but there are a number of technical items yet to be improved and bugs to be fixed on various platforms. As a failsafe, you should have an alternate means of connecting with the event organizer. At ELO, for instance, we set up all panelists with a text-based group chat so that everyone can still communicate, in the event that something goes wrong with our video call.

10. It's always a good idea to work closely with the organizers of an online event and listen to their requests and recommendations. It seems obvious, but I know from experience that it doesn't always happen. At ELO we have a "Guide for Presenters" that we provide to all speakers. The problem is that speakers sometimes make assumptions about what is necessary based on their own past, generalized experiences—so they don't actually read what we sent them. Others do read the guide, but simply prefer to do their presentation their own way. These approaches are a sure way to avoid getting invited back and receiving referrals. Instead of doing this, always follow the guidelines offered by event organizers. They are trying to make the presenters look good.

11. It is sometimes useful to use a "polling function" at the start of the session. This allows organizers to get audience feedback and

discern which subject matter is of greatest interest, so that the most relevant questions can be posed first.

12. There can be an ongoing "chat" for the attendees during a presentation. This can be an excellent gauge of audience feedback. You, as the presenter, are not required to monitor the chat or reply, but someone other than the presenter should monitor it and record key feedback for later reference.

13. If you can access an elevated monitor, it's a good idea to stand when you are presenting. Standing generally allows a speaker to convey more energy and motion, and allows for more natural movement and body language. If you are using a green screen, make sure to move your hands more slowly and deliberately.

14. Murphy's Law (see Law #29) holds true all over the world and in all communication formats. What can go wrong, may go wrong. All of the above methods to deliver an excellent webinar are subject to the possibility of something going wrong! There may be events beyond your control, such as garbled voices, a disconnection, power outages, etc. In the event of unforeseen circumstances, try your best to continue. Remember the basic principle of every presentation: "The Show Must Go On!"

LAW #34: In order to be a great online panelist and webinar presenter, one must have an ongoing commitment to learning. The rules evolve along with the technology. Don't be left behind.

C.35: BUSINESS & BOARD MEETINGS

Many individuals reading this book will be part of business and board meetings via video call. Of course, these situations are not public speaking per se, but they do require you to communicate publicly with a group of people, and you need to do your best. As part of my work with ELO, I have organized many video business and board meetings. I offer the following guidelines as a set of "best practices" to make a video meeting as productive as possible. You may already be familiar with the below pointers; if so, treat this information as a "refresher."

Eye Contact—Try to look into the camera and not at yourself on the screen, no matter how good you think you look! This will allow you to communicate most effectively with everyone else when speaking. If you are looking sideways, or in various other directions, it creates an instant disconnect with the audience.

Positioning—Within reason, the closer your face is to the monitor the better—this is much more engaging for the audience. The further back that someone is seated, the harder it becomes to make out facial expressions and the more the personal connection is diminished. If you are seated at your desk, you should be leaning into the monitor at a distance of 2–3 feet (for example, think of the positioning of speakers and panelists on CNN), not sitting away from your desk or slouching in your chair. Elevate your monitor on your table so that your face is on an even level, rather than having the monitor facing upwards, distorting your face and inviting viewers to do a virtual nostril inspection.

Volume—Make sure you can be clearly heard. Do a sound check before you get started. The problem with meeting participants is rarely their microphone (unless they forget to unmute themselves), but rather the fact that they are sitting too far back, or turned away from the microphone. It's hard to communicate well if other people in the meeting cannot hear you clearly. Further, make sure that you have no background noise when presenting. I have stopped a webinar presenter previously because there was too much chatter from a nearby conversation.

Mute Yourself—Make sure that you mute yourself when the meeting is in progress and someone is presenting. Otherwise, the background noise or chatter can be quite distracting—and it is often louder than you think it is.

Body Language—Be mindful of your body language. If you are looking sideways during a meeting and people are seeing your profile, that communicates that you are not interested in being part of the meeting, whether or not that is your intent. Be careful with your hand movements, as well; do not wave your hands in front of your camera, as they will appear grotesquely over-sized, and if you are using a green screen, remember that your hands will blur when they are moved rapidly. Instead, move your head slightly and have positive facial expressions. Put your hands flat on your desk, beside your monitor and out of sight. Lastly, someone probably told you this in Kindergarten: don't put your hands in front of your mouth when talking. Not a good technique if you wish to communicate.

Distractions & Focus—If you want to be part of a meeting, then you need to focus and be present. If you think you can multitask—work the keyboard while participating, send emails, make calls, text, etc.—well, you can't. You may think you're hiding it, but no one else is fooled. Similarly, always make sure that your cell phone and email alerts are turned off.

Device—The best device to use for a video call is a laptop on a desk. I have had cases where someone joins a meeting via smartphone while doing something else, like walking a dog in the park. When that happens, the image bounces along, the phone gets dropped, and all in all, it does not come across as very professional.

Presence—If you want to be part of a meeting, you need to have both your audio and video on. If the meeting involves a person presenting to a large group, there is no need for audience members to have their video on, but if you intend to participate in a business meeting, you need to have your video on at all times. Assume that as soon as you get started, you are on-screen at all times (meaning it's not possible to "sneak out" and grab a coffee at any point!).

Dual Display—It's helpful to use two monitors, when possible. This setup will allow you to have one monitor displaying your group of participants, and the other dedicated to your notes or documents.

Lighting—Be very mindful of the lighting in your room. An overhead light fixture or a desk lamp may appear very bright in the background, or a wide-open window right behind you, when the sun suddenly appears, may be far too bright. Be careful to avoid lighting that makes you look like a glowing extraterrestrial or a blank silhouette! I recommend using a "ring light," which is often mounted on a tripod and casts an even light onto the presenter. The ring light reduces shadows in the face while illuminating the eyes.

Background—An artificial background for video calls can be helpful or distracting. A nice office with some bookshelves can work well. Sometimes people have a drab wall or their backyard behind them. On the other hand, sometimes you can see a table with a few objects lying on it behind a speaker, which can be distracting as the viewers try to determine what those objects could be. If you don't have great options for a natural background, use a virtual one. Another advantage of a virtual background is that you can include your company logo. The bottom line is that the focus should remain on the speakers and their message.

Raise Hand—Many programs provide a "raised hand" icon or equivalent option on the toolbar along the edge of your screen. Especially with larger meetings, using this tool can be very helpful. The moderator can see who wishes to speak next, which avoids the common problem of people speaking simultaneously or over one another due to a time delay.

LAW #35: In order effectively participate in business and board meetings, one needs to understand the basic dynamics of communicating well in a digital environment.

D—THE APPLICATIONS

D.36: INTRODUCTIONS

There is more than one type of introduction, and thus this chapter is divided into three sections: introducing yourself; being introduced; and introducing others.

Introducing Yourself

One of the most important introductions you give may be the one you provide for yourself. I am not referring to situations where you are an invited speaker, but rather at various business gatherings. For example, I was recently at a business event for about 25 people, few of whom were familiar with one another. As a simple icebreaker, the host said, "Please stand up, provide your name and company, and say one interesting thing about yourself." Despite how simple this request is, at the same time, the process is quite revealing. It shows how people present themselves, and reveals whether they are articulate, confident, able to follow instructions, and capable of thinking on their feet. I have routinely witnessed people failing to take this icebreaker too seriously, which often results in others returning the favor and not taking them seriously, either.

As noted in Law #3, others will typically assess you within one minute. At this particular event, most people's introductions were inarticulate, full of disjointed remarks, and failing to address the handful of questions the host asked. One person even used profanity, which I imagine was his normal speaking style (see Law #20).

123

A short self-introduction is also a bit of an ego-meter. You can see instantly how self-absorbed people are when they talk for way too long, making it all about them, not the event. On the other hand, even how people stand up is revealing. Many people at the event I attended stood awkwardly, shifting from side to side and looking very uncomfortable. When you introduce yourself, stand straight, feet slightly apart, shoulders square, looking directly at the group, using hand gestures appropriately. Treat it like a mini-speech.

A similar occasion for people to introduce themselves takes place at the ELO Forums. We have a VIP Reception prior to each event with 30 or so supporters. I always have everyone introduce themselves: name, company, and the business they are in. I have had over 60 events and we have had VIP Receptions at most of them, so, I have heard well over 1,000 people do short introductions of themselves. I always remind people that we have limited time and we want to include everyone. The best speakers do the following: stick to the instructions; remain clear and concise; stay upbeat; and reflect confidence, poise, and class.

Being Introduced

Elsewhere in this book I talk about how to start effectively in terms of using a hook (Law #4) and managing the most dangerous 15 seconds (Law #21), but I want to address this particular issue specifically.

Say you have been asked to speak at an event. Your name, background, and the title of your talk have been promoted to the constituency. At the event, depending upon the size, there may be a program which repeats that information. At the event, your name, background, and the title of your talk are given again in the introduction immediately before you head up to the podium.

The wrong thing for you to do next would be to say, "Hi, I'm John Smith, President of John Smith Enterprises, and I will talk about *Lessons on Innovation in the Widget Industry*." You are repeating what everyone knows, and instantly losing the audience.

Everyone knows who you are. Instead make sure you start immediately with a hook. Say something like, "Let me take you back to my house in New York on the morning of 9/11. I was chatting with my wife and four young kids as I was about to leave for my office in the World Trade Center. My career was reaching new peaks. I was ready for another great day of living the American dream…"

When you are speaking somewhere new, I find that it is a good practice to confirm with the event organizer exactly what your introducer will be saying about you. I have witnessed many bungled introductions of myself over the years. Sometimes people are working off an old CV—you are introduced as working for a company you have long since left. Perhaps your introducer has cherry-picked part of your CV, highlighting only secondary points. The most common mistake is mispronouncing a person's name. In my case, it's a particular challenge. It's a Dutch name, pronounced as "Go-sen" and not "Goose-en." The sweetest sound in any language is one's own name—and, I would add, one's own name pronounced correctly. In some cases, I have been introduced by a person reading out my CV. My own approach is for an introduction of myself to be brief. Your presentation and not your CV will establish your credibility. Also, long introductions sometimes feel like a wedge being driven between me and the audience; it then takes more effort to draw people back in to connect with you.

Introducing Others

How hard can it be to introduce someone else? Apparently, much harder than one might think. Again, the basic rules of public speaking apply: remember the context, and be prepared. Many introductions are bungled simply because people are not prepared to make them.

Over the past 15 years, I have hosted more than 200 speakers for ELO conferences. Typically, I introduce the speakers in the simplest way possible. I usually know them, I am familiar with their background, and since I am the organizer of the event, I know the overall context.

One year, I had the bright idea to get more people involved in the program. I began to look for people who would be appropriate to do introductions of various presenters. I buttonholed introducers on the day of the event and without enough guidance. I soon realized that my motivation to get more people involved had misfired. An introduction should be treated like a mini speech.

When doing an introduction, you should get detailed instructions from the person you are introducing and/or the host. Depending upon the event, there may have been a speaker bio on the website leading up to the conference, and the bio may also be in a conference brochure. In this case, you don't need to run through the credentials to introduce the speaker. Simply say the speaker's name, position, the title of the talk, and the speaker's home city or country.

In some cases, such as with a keynote speaker, you may wish to read through a number of the credentials. Mentioning a speaker's credentials is a good way to remind people why they have come to hear this particular person speak. Or the speaker may have something specific that they wish to have you highlight, such as a recently published book.

Again, remember that it's not about you when you go up to do an introduction. Don't say, "Well, uhm, I don't know Bob, in fact have never met Bob, in fact had never heard of Bob, but I'm pleased to introduce Bill, uh, I mean Bob." Instead, ooze class. "Hi, it's my pleasure to introduce our next speaker, Bob, President of Smith Inc., New York City. You can find his bio in the conference brochure. I'm very much looking forward to his presentation." Make it professional, succinct, and get off the stage—you are the only thing standing between the presenter and the audience.

Sometimes people try to get cute with their introduction. They want to find some little-known fact about the person they are introducing— something that might be interesting, but which is usually irrelevant. "Did you know that our next presenter was once almost eaten by a crocodile?" an introducer might say. That doesn't have anything to do with the presentation, though. Instead, try something like, "Our next presenter is founder of X Co, which just recently won a prize for innovation that was just announced a few days ago. She will be speaking about how she and her team developed that innovative product."

As always, be careful about the details when you're preparing to introduce a speaker. Make sure that you get the facts straight: the person's proper title, the name of the company, and the proper pronunciation of a speaker's name. Remember that if you are doing an introduction, it's not about you—it's about the person you are introducing.

You also need to be very careful with what you say when do introductions. I was emceeing one of our ELO Forums, and the first few speakers were very good. As I was introducing the next speaker, I made an on-the-fly comment along the lines of, "It just keeps getting better." I was implying that the event was getting positive momentum because of the aggregation of excellent speakers. One of the first speakers came up to me later to express his annoyance, saying I had implied that he was not as good as the subsequent speakers. The bottom line: be very careful what you say.

LAW #36: Demonstrate your class and professionalism by mastering the art of a good introduction in all contexts: introducing yourself, being introduced, and introducing others.

D.37: BEING AN EMCEE

There is no greater opportunity for a person to play the fool than when they are emceeing a wedding. It is a Shakespearean witch's brew of circumstances ripe for disaster. There is commonly an inexperienced emcee, who typically got the opportunity because of some relation to the engaged couple rather than any skill. There are inexperienced event organizers: the wedding party and their families, who generally provide the emcee with few guidelines. In fact, the emcee is often left to organize many details of the program. This is a bit like putting Al Capone in charge of the IRS.

The environment itself can also pose a threat to professionalism. Many at the wedding are in a happy, loose-lipped mood, seemingly inspiring the emcee to act the same. The attendees' collective guard is down. To top it all off, there is often the social lubricant of alcohol and the open bar. The potential for verbal missteps is often heightened by the fact that, while the newlyweds are presumably compatible, the two families may be like Shakespeare's Montagues and Capulets. I have witnessed many weddings and I cannot think of a context where I have seen more laws of public speaking breached at once.

One memorable wedding had the uncle of the groom emceeing. He was a middle-aged medical doctor, and throughout the wedding he was determined to make sure the audience knew that he was really good at his craft. He clearly hated toiling in the relative anonymity of his medical practice. His opportunity to emcee was his moment of glory.

The wedding was about the bride and groom—and him. He used his time onstage to wallow in feeling his oats. He also apparently thought he would ingratiate himself with his new friends, the bride's family, but he went about it very badly. Many of them had come from a different part of the country with long, cold winters, humid summers, and not much in between. He effectively painted the bride's family as a cross between country nincompoops and small-town hicks. He rubbed it in at every interlude. "All in good humor," he apparently thought. No one else agreed.

The upside for him: you don't know what you don't know. The emcee paraded around the wedding buffet, quite pleased with himself, ready to accept congratulatory back slaps which never came, and available for photos which were never snapped. In short, he was memorable for years to come as an unmitigated disaster. There was too much of a focus on him and his ineptitude.

Here's another example. Often weddings have young emcees, as they are typically the best man, maid of honor, or peers of the wedding party. The problem is that younger people's concept of funny may not equal that of many of the guests. Weddings are unique in that the age range of audience members, and thus their tastes, are often quite varied.

In particular, how people define what qualifies as "crude" can vary widely. Does the emcee use the reference point of what grandma will laugh at, or the parents, or the 20-something wedding party? There's one way to find out. On one memorable occasion, two young co-emcees were sharing the podium to make a few remarks about the groom.

They were chortling to themselves as they bumbled up to the podium, guffawing so hard they could barely get the words out. They reminded the bride that her other half likes hunting. "But watch out!" they warned the bride. "He likes to sleep with his rifle" (they didn't explain whether or not it was loaded). Then they laughed even more. "So, when you're sleeping together, if you feel something very long and hard, well, ha ha, that's his rifle and not something else." Then they burst out laughing.

The spectacle of these two young jokers was treated by the audience the same way one would look at an accident on the highway: somewhat detached, wondering what just happened. All of us looked at the bride and groom, and they were frozen like, well, a moose in the headlights. These emcees were asked because they were friends—not because they knew how to handle themselves in front of people. They did, however, succeed in making the remarks of the bride and groom look that much better by comparison.

Being a good emcee requires a keen understanding of the public speaking laws of success. This book covers everything you need to be a good emcee, and most importantly, to help you honor the wedded couple and their families.

Ask yourself: what is the purpose of the event? What do the newlyweds want? Who is the audience? Remember that the event is not about you as the emcee. Don't do anything to focus attention on yourself. You are there to serve the audience. Your mark of success will be if no one remembers you were the emcee.

One final note regarding the role of emcees. If you have dual emcees, don't allow them to cross-introduce each other, or be very careful to do it properly. I was once at a university sports banquet that had co-emcees. In that situation, it turned out that twice as many emcees was twice as bad. The emcees were a coach and a former athlete, respectively, and in a failed attempt at modesty, they opted to introduce each other. "Let me introduce Coach So-and-So," began the athlete. She went on and on about his accomplishments, great and small, until it was cringe inducing. We were about to recover from this sycophantic escapade when the coach said, "Let me now introduce my co-emcee." The whole affair began again. These co-introductions chiefly served to signal that we were off to a long display of self-congratulatory preening. Shameless boasting masquerading as mutual introductions only displays a huge lack of class, confidence and professionalism for all to see.

LAW #37: An emcee's role is to facilitate the success of an event and not be the focus of it. When people remember the emcee, it's typically only for the wrong reasons.

D.38: THE OPEN MIC

You may be tempted to jump at the opportunity of an "open mic," which typically presents itself in a few different contexts. Most commonly, after a presentation, the organizers may put a stand up mic in the aisle of the ballroom. People can walk up to the mic, get in line, and ask the presenter their questions. Remember that how you ask a question will reflect on you in terms of professionalism and likeability. The best approach is to ask a question that is on point and well-constructed.

Unfortunately, this is not always the case. Commonly, the person posing a question is using the open mic as a platform to promote an unrelated interest. "Hello, this is John Smith of Smith Enterprises. We are the top widget maker in the country, if not the world, and possibly beyond. In fact, our widgets have a number of excellent features and, now that I think about it, you can get them at various outlets. In fact, we have a 2-for-1 special right now, with operators standing by. Anyways, I had an interesting experience with one of our distributors. You see, we have this contract, which has a clause that allows the buyer to reject the widgets on the basis that…" and so on, and so on, until Mr. Smith finally concludes with, "What do you think about what I have just explained?" Often the speaker will need to ask, "What was the question exactly?"

This kind of situation is why the "open mic" is a dying species. The open mic becomes a platform for too many people to be inconsiderate. The idea is you are asking a question of the speaker related to the presentation, and not using it as a platform for your own views. I no longer provide an "open mic" at our ELO Forums, as things can easily go awry. The present approach at our ELO Forums works well. We often do a Q&A with speakers. I, as the emcee, have my cellphone with me and we put my phone number on the screen, inviting people to text me their questions.

In this way, I can screen the questions and see which are most relevant and appropriate. The questions as I read them are also carefully worded and succinct. This has proven to be an effective way to handle many questions.

Another common context of an open mic is that of weddings and funerals. In both instances, it has minimal upside but great potential for disaster. After a memorial service, for example, the attendees will typically gather in a separate venue, or the church basement, for a light meal and a short program. The officiant and the family will share their thoughts and memories. Afterwards, there will often be an open mic. Where I come from, this is called "freiwilliges," which is German for "voluntary contribution," or, more colloquially, a "free for all."

On the one hand there is the positive side. People from the extended circle of family and friends have the opportunity to give congratulations, well wishes, or sympathy, as the case may be. Of course, with the risks associated with an open mic, I find it better to schedule such speakers into the program, or else let them say their piece privately—but, for better or worse, the open mic persists.

On the other hand there is the downside. Here are two examples of an open mic gone wrong. At one funeral I attended, a lady with a black hat walked up from the back of the room. "Hello, I'm Madalene Wiltshire. I am the lady in the black hat. I knew Gertrude, but not that well. Actually, we weren't that close and didn't talk much. I was in the same neighborhood. I lived ten houses down the street, on the same side, in the beautiful big house with the nice wrought-iron fence. In fact, it's for sale. As I was saying, I didn't know her that well, and in fact I don't know the family well, but I wish you all the best." It was clear to everyone there that Ms. Wiltshire saw the open mic as an opportunity to hear herself talk more than to honor the deceased.

Another example at a funeral wasn't quite disastrous, but it was certainly odd. The open mic session in the church basement was underway, and a few people—some relatives and close friends—had already come and gone, shared great memories. Then, from the back of the room, a casually-dressed young lady who looked to be in her late teens came forward.

"Hello, I'm Sally," she whimpered. "No one here knows me. I was doing the sound controls at the back of the room. I didn't know Mary. In fact, I had never heard of Mary. I don't actually know any of Mary's family. But listening to everyone talk about her, I just want to come up and say that it sounds like she was an amazing lady." Was that something that needed to be said in front of 200 people? Why not say it to someone privately? It was almost like having a passerby see that a memorial service was going on and pop into the church to say a few words.

In short, all the basic public speaking rules apply to the open mic. Ask yourself: what's the purpose of speaking here? What's the context? Can it be helpful to the grieving family? Remember, it's not about you. It's about them. The open mic can be a great thing, so if you decide to make your move, just remember those rules.

LAW #38: Beware of the pitfalls of the open mic. If you have the option, don't do it. If you are not in control, but merely assigned to monitor the event, then do so very carefully.

D.39: SPONTANEOUS COMBUSTION

Some of the greatest opportunities to separate yourself from the pack and have your moment of glory are the spontaneous ones. I have had a lot of spontaneous opportunities over the years, and they can work well to your advantage. The situations in which such opportunities arise vary. Often, one can be at a gathering and be suddenly asked to say something or to introduce oneself. One of the few things I remember from high school science class besides the Periodic Table is the phrase "spontaneous combustion." You want to light up the room rather than go up in smoke.

A few years back, I was at one of my extended family Christmas gatherings, which typically include over 100 people. This year an aunt and uncle were hosting. After a customary meal of more desserts than entrees, we moved on to rest of the loosely described program, which included some four-part harmonies, family updates, and the like. As we plunked ourselves down in our chairs, my uncle started his emceeing. After some introductory greetings, he then said, "Now Rick will come up and share some thoughts on Christmas."

The first I heard about my involvement in the program was the same time as everyone else! I instantly sprung up, and in the 10 seconds spent walking to the podium, I organized my thoughts. On the one hand, I could have refused to get up, and simply shouted back, "No thanks, I didn't know about this!"

On the other hand, this was a family gathering, and the thought had popped into my uncle's head on the spur of the moment. My reaction was to go with the flow. Although it was a personal rather than business setting, it's always good to sound reasonably intelligible. To the family members gathered, it seemed like it was planned. I came up with some structured remarks before making my exit.

The key in that situation, as any spontaneous scenario, is to quickly adopt a bit of a structure. Ask yourself, "(1) What's the main point? (2) What's the context?" Then, make up (3) an introduction, (4) a body, and (5) a conclusion. I went up there and said how much I appreciate these gatherings, told a story from a past gathering, and concluded by saying, "It's great to be here, and thanks, Aunt and Uncle, for hosting this year." It sounds simple, but it's more challenging when you are thrown for a loop. Don't get up there and start talking with no beginning or end. Instead, those five key points will stand you in good stead.

Apart from personal situations, there are many times in a business context when you will need to speak spontaneously in front of a group of people gathered around you at a cocktail reception or a dozen people in a board room. Let's say you are having drinks and mingling about prior to an evening dinner event. You are with five or six people. Someone asks, "So, what do you do?" Another scenario is when you go to a business meeting, perhaps working on a deal with a number of parties. You are there to provide your particular expertise. Then, someone says, so what do you do exactly? You now have the floor. A boardroom full of people now are looking forward to your answer. You then have a great opportunity to articulately and convincingly explain what you do. In the majority of cases, people can't explain what they themselves do. They bungle their own introduction. It's as if they have never been asked that question or never thought that they would need to provide an explanation. Instead, you need to be ready.

Your ability to deliver spontaneous remarks effectively is a great opportunity, because it will separate you from the pack. Most people are not prepared and cannot effectively deliver prepared remarks along with thinking on their feet. This skill is delivering under pressure. Being able to do that will show your true mettle.

LAW #39: Always be prepared for spontaneous speaking opportunities by having a sense of structure and purpose, so that you burn brightly rather than going up in smoke.

D.40: BUSINESS PRESENTATIONS

Business presentations are a modified form of public speaking. They are not performances, nor do they allow for a set piece. At the same time, though, the focus is on communicating a message in an effective manner. You are imparting information, and you want to do it successfully.

The scope of business gatherings includes both internal and external meetings. People sometimes don't take internal meetings as seriously, as if presenting to their colleagues didn't merit the same attention to detail and professionalism as a public gathering. That's a big mistake. Everyone at the meeting will be forming an impression of how you conduct yourself. If you are not able to act professionally and present articulately to your business team, then you may not be ready an external audience.

When you are meeting with outside groups, the same dynamics apply. It is vital that you adhere to all the public speaking rules of success. People are always instinctively assessing your competency. A lack of skill implies a lack of training, and this will reflect on your company, too.

In the context of a sales call, the biggest challenge is to avoid the "show up and throw up" presentation model. For many businesspeople, the idea is to "show up and deliver the presentation that I have prepared." "Mission accomplished," then, means that the speaker has successfully shown up, delivered the entire presentation, and done it in about the time allocated. Unfortunately, all this might still be for naught. Think of it like a sales presentation. The objective is not to get through your entire pitch—the objective is to make a sale. The important questions are: was the presentation effective? Did people understand the message? Were they engaged? Did the speaker establish a connection with the listeners?

Rarely should you hold questions until the end of a business meeting. If people are engaged and want to ask questions soon after you get going, let them. You may think that it will disrupt your presentation, but that mentality is missing the point. The purpose of your presentation is to communicate with them. Insisting questions wait until the end means people may forget the question, or you will simply lose the context for it. Also, leaving the questions for the end implies that the questions are a bit of an addendum, an afterthought, whereas the goal in any presentation is to make the audience your priority.

I approach business presentations as something dynamic. I go into them with the idea that I will lead a group through a discussion, but make sure I am also ready to change direction. I never lose sight of my main objectives, which are to get engagement from the listeners and communicate with them effectively. I have done investor presentations where I will get bombarded with questions and answer a succession of them—and fail to get through or barely even start my slideshow presentation. That's fine. My objective was not to get through all the slides. My objective is to communicate an idea.

LAW #40: Business presentations are about communication and engagement, rather than simply delivering information.

D.41: HANDS-ON PRESENTATION

Sometimes you may be called on to do what I refer to as a "hands-on presentation." In these situations, you are not just speaking: you are demonstrating. This is still a public session, but the dynamics are different from a "normal presentation." While I was living in Hong Kong, I developed a guide for navigating this kind of unconventional presentation. My usual custom while working in Hong Kong was to have breakfast meetings with various businesspeople, often out-of-towners who were visiting Hong Kong. My favorite meeting place was the main dining room of the famed Mandarin Hotel, typically ranked in the top ten hotels of the world. It was a very nice room, laid out comfortably and conducive to quiet conversations.

The service was superb and downright legendary. My favorite memory of the service was that one time I was shuffling papers and one slipped to the side of the table, over the edge, and was wafting towards the ground. From out of nowhere, with rapier like speed, a server lunged for it and caught it before it hit the ground. That was worth the breakfast right there.

One fellow I invited to join me for breakfast was Gordon Redding, who was at that time a professor and the dean of the School of Business at the University of Hong Kong. During one of our breakfasts, he asked me if I could do a session for a handful of his MBA students on "The Art of the Power Breakfast." It might have sounded silly, and I had never done this type of session previously, but as soon as he mentioned it, I realized that his idea made a lot of sense. It tied right into the importance of social skills and emotional intelligence for the future success of his students.

I agreed, and we planned the session for about eight students, plus Gordon and myself. We booked a couple of tables in a discreet corner of the Mandarin Hotel restaurant. This was not the kind of situation that would work with a formal presentation, but the same basic rules applied. I asked myself: "What's the context? What's the point? What's the best way to get the message across? How can I best interact with the students?" As with any presentation, all of the same dynamics were at play: I wanted to do a great job for the organizer (Gordon Redding) and the audience (the students). I wanted to have a positive impact. I wanted to come across in a credible and professional manner.

In this kind of situation, I recommend treating a restaurant as a private club. I would generally sit in the same spot: a table in the corner, with a sight line to the entrance so I could spot my guests coming. Sitting in the corner minimizes the chance of distractions of people walking by your table. Often my guests would be people I hadn't previously met; always make sure that the host or server knows your name and those of your guests.

Don't talk too loudly. Don't be paranoid, but you never know who else is within earshot. I was once having lunch in a different restaurant in Hong Kong, where tables and seats were generally quite close together. I was sitting back-to-back with another table, mere inches away. Soon enough, I discovered that the table behind me was one of our direct competitors meeting with an out-of-town guest. It was quite interesting to be a fly on the wall for that conversation. Don't be overly suspicious, but at the same time, don't assume you know who else is within earshot at these meetings.

Ironically, even if you are at a restaurant, the meeting is not about the food. Order your food and get it out of the way. Stay away from buffets, as it's disruptive, and order something that you can eat with minimal theatrics—this is easier at breakfast.

Etiquette is important. On the one hand, you are not having dinner with the Queen, and likely do not have to keep multiple knives and forks straight. At the same time, you don't want to look out of place. I still remember one of my contacts using his bread to wipe up the gravy on his dinner plate. I actually thought his next move was going to be to put the plate to his face and start licking it. You can undermine your credibility if you look like you don't get out of the house much.

Here are some basics that I relayed to the students, which will help you look like you are ready for prime time.

1. BMW: bread on the left, meal (plate) in the center and water (drinks) on the right. When you are at a round banquet table and the cutlery and plates are crammed together, use the correct plate. During my first week at McGill Law School ten of us went for dinner with a professor. We were seated at a small round table. I unknowingly used the wrong bread plate. It threw off the whole table. Someone loudly blurted out, "who took the wrong plate?!" I felt instantly exposed as a blue collar pretender among private school educated progeny of professionals. Look and act like you are ready for prime time.

2. Your cutlery is not a weapon. Don't hold your knife and fork while you're giving directions or gesticulating. It's more common (although still not OK) at family gatherings, but this behavior is definitely to be avoided in a business context. Besides looking silly, you may prompt other people to hold their plates in self-defense, lest they be pierced by a utensil!

3. Your food is not a lollipop. Only what you can fit on your fork goes in your mouth. Don't put the entire sausage on your fork, for instance, nibbling away at it. If you want to provide comic relief and are a part-time clown, perhaps you can take this tack, but otherwise cut it up into bite-sized pieces on your plate.

4. Don't talk with your mouth full of food. This seems quite basic. We can all wait until you swallow, and no one wants that visual stuck in anyone's mind.

5. Be considerate. Make sure you're ready to pass things to others at the table. If you are with a guest at a table, make sure you ask if they need refills. Think of yourself as being a good host, even when you aren't at home.

6. Be clear on who is the host and who's paying. Typically the person selecting the restaurant and making the reservation is the host and should pay, especially when it is a business situation. When it's

peers, friends, or associates, it can get murky—when in doubt, clear it up in advance.

7. Lift the food to your mouth. Don't plant your head in your plate.

8. Be appropriate with the servers and all staff. This approach seems obvious, but it doesn't reflect well on you if you are rude to staff. At the same time, I often see the reverse situation. Don't be too chatty with servers. You are not trying to be their friend or add them to your social media universe. Maintain focus on the guests you're meeting with.

It's not a surprise that most interview processes for a professional job opportunity involve a meeting over a meal at a restaurant. In short, these various guidelines are quite important.

LAW #41: A successful hands-on presentation over a meal, requires the practice of the basic rules of etiquette.

D.42: CHAIRING A BOARD MEETING

"Professor Smith, please restate your point." "Professor Jones, did you wish to respond to Professor Smith." I watched the chair of the meeting of about 150 professors with a mixture of fascination and pure awe. I had never seen anything like it—before or since.

I was in the middle of my time studying at the McGill Law School. I decide to run as the student representative for the Faculty of Law at the University Senate. I wanted to do something in student politics, and my predecessor convinced me that I would likely run unopposed and get in (he was right), and that the meetings included coffee and cookies (right again). So, I figured that I could serve the common good, boost my CV, and get a sugar fix at the same time: an ideal student trifecta.

The University Senate comprised about 150 faculty members, and the meetings were chaired by David Johnston, the University Principal. My objective was to say nothing, and enjoy the cookies and the proceedings in equal measure. I did, however, learn a valuable lesson that has stuck with me. I have never to this day seen anyone run a meeting better than David Johnston.

David Johnston is no ordinary fellow. He served as Governor General of Canada from 2010 to 2017. He studied at Harvard University and, later, the University of Cambridge. He went on to work as a professor at various post-secondary institutions in Canada. David Johnston was Principal of McGill for 10 years and then at the law school for 5 years. In 2010, he was appointed governor general. While at Harvard, he captained the varsity ice hockey team and met and befriended Erich Segal, the two becoming jogging partners. In 1970, Segal wrote the best-selling novel *Love Story*, basing a character in the book—Davey, a captain of the hockey team—on Johnston. He has been awarded 36 honorary doctorates, thus far.

Watching David Johnston chair the Faculty Senate meetings was a thing of beauty. He was diplomatic and dignified. He was very careful about making sure that everyone was heard, that their position was articulated clearly, and that they had their full say—while also staying on point. He would scour the room for people who wanted to speak, seeking clarification when necessary. He would make sure everything was on schedule and on topic, and he would focus and listen to whoever was speaking.

While I was working in Hong Kong, Principal Johnson regularly made trips to "fly the university flag" overseas. Fortunately, I had the opportunity to meet him in Hong Kong a couple of times. He was as charismatic in person as he was as the chair of meetings. He was dignified, polite, and a very good listener.

His skill did not go unnoticed outside the university context, either. Johnston has moderated several televised leaders' debates in Canada. He further served on various corporate boards of directors, and he is the only non-American citizen to chair the Harvard Board of Overseers.

Johnston was quite amazing to watch, especially as a law student. I could see that his key skills were directed towards realizing the context. This was a meeting with a lot of people, whose time was valuable and whose attention was short. There were important things to get done, and it was clear that he was there to facilitate involvement, and not to be the center of attention or dominate the meeting. I think it was clear that he had an innate sense of equity. While David Johnston had a number of unique personal qualities, much of what he did to be successful can be learned and emulated.

As part of my consulting practice I am often involved in corporate governance. A starting point for success is to have a competent chair, like Johnston above. A good chair has to be able to do a couple of things, all rooted in the public speaking laws of success. On the one hand, there are the mechanics: there needs to be a clear agenda, which is distributed in advance with any supporting documents, and the proper items need to be on the agenda. The focus of the meeting is on strategic, not operational, concerns. You can't run a proper meeting if you are bogged down with the details. Then there needs to be proper notetaking and a record of action items.

The other half—and the challenge—is the execution. The chair needs to make sure everyone is heard and that they stay on point. If you let people ramble on too long, the meeting will soon go sideways. The chair needs to ensure that people are making an appropriate point, and encourage them to do so effectively.

I was on the board of a non-profit organization that was chaired by a landscaper—and it turned out that he was better in the garden than in the boardroom. He was a very genial fellow, and his approach seemed to be to let everyone talk as much as they wanted in the hope that they would eventually find a point. He was a people-pleaser, loath to ask anyone to be uncharacteristically concise. The meetings would typically go 30 minutes over the limit. To him, it didn't seem to matter much. We discussed too many operational issues, too much time was given for people who were unprepared to speak, and the culture seemed to promote letting everyone add their voice, but not their insight, into the equation. I soon found a way to get off the board.

The chair sets a tone and a culture to the board operation. If a chair is too passive, the board is likely to become inefficient. It also discourages people who could positively contribute to this situation. Often, they end up leaving. I always advise anyone who is asked to be on a board to attend and observe a board meeting before making a decision. Doing this will make your decision much easier.

LAW #42: Being able to chair a meeting well have a huge positive impact, for both the board members and the organization.

D.43: THE INTERVIEW

You may have an opportunity to interview people, in small or large forums, for work or other purposes. Conducting an interview well is no easy feat. As with anything, doing it well makes it look easy. I recently saw a great example of how not to do an interview. I watched an interview on YouTube. I looked up a certain speaker. One of the top 10 links that came up was an interview with this speaker conducted by a magazine writer. The person would ask a question, and then cut off the answer with reminiscences of how that related to their own experience. The problem was that I was not interested in what the interviewer had to say.

To do a great interview requires mastery of some basic pointers. First, ask well-chosen questions, and do so succinctly. A good question hits the mark; ask the question, and then shut up! Your job is to listen. Doing interviews can be exciting, as the magic happens while the interview is underway. You are listening to the answer to see if there are follow up questions you can ask. It is not a matter of getting through your ten questions in sequence. Often the best questions and the best moments happen as a result of something that is said during the course of the interview.

When you are doing an interview, nobody cares what you think. Let me repeat: no one cares what you think. Get used to it. If you are doing an interview, you must have the confidence to realize that you are there to facilitate someone else's insights. Get back to the basics. Is the purpose for you to pull out the insights of the particular guest? If so, then proceed carefully. If your objective is to have an excuse to talk about yourself, that's different.

Good interviewers ask a question and then listen. They speak methodically. There are interested in the answer. They give the interviewee space and time to speak. There are plenty of great examples of excellent interviewers; in previous years it was Barbara Walters, or Larry King (most of the time). An excellent reference source is the CBS TV Show "60 Minutes." The episodes are generally the most informative and best packaged 13 minute interviews in TV all week. CBS has a wellspring of great interviewers. They ask great questions—and then listen. Despite having watched all these interviews, we as listeners don't really know much about the interviewers. That's the point. Their skill is in getting the interviewees to talk.

One critical aspect of an interview is to not be judgmental. Ask the question, and then let the answer come. Even if the response reveals something that is reprehensible to the interviewer, don't launch into condemnation. The viewers can do that on their own. Your job is not to give your opinion. Your role is to get the information out. At most, the interviewer might ask a more pointed question.

Another important aspect of an interview is to have the skill to ask the questions that people would want answered. If you were interviewing Barack Obama you might ask, "What was it like to realize that you were going to become the first African-American president in US history?" You wouldn't say, "Is it true that you don't like onions on your burger?"

If you can do interviews well, you will make the interviewee look good. You can lead the conversation, get your guest to clarify and re-emphasize points, and bring out their best qualities.

A short while ago, I was at a university sports banquet and the keynote speaker was a well-known hockey player, the proverbial enforcer, pugilist, on-ice cop, in other words, "the goon." I met him at the pre-banquet reception. He was quite bright and articulate.

The event organizers had asked him to do a 20-minute keynote. He had about 3 minutes of content that he vigorously punched through for 20 minutes. He didn't know what people wanted to hear, so he basically went in circles until his time was up. He came across as an affable guy off the ice, who was focused on the ice, without a whole lot to say. The main benefit was simply to see him. That guy was huge, with fists like ham hocks. That's what an "NHL goon" looks like.

Instead of asking him to make up a keynote speech, an interview format would have been perfect for both him and the audience. He would have come across much better. An interviewer could have drawn out his humor, and led him to talk about on-ice rivalries and key events in his life. They could have focused on the challenges of even getting to the NHL, the risks of concussions and injuries, etc.

I have done hundreds of interviews with business leaders and well-known personalities, such as Mark Burnett (as referred to in Law #13). The key is to make it clear that you are working with the interviewee. You want them to look good and do their best. You are not doing an exposé. I will typically prepare a list of questions and then let the interviewee know that I might deviate from the script, depending upon their answers.

As an interviewer, you need to understand the context of an interview. Often people don't realize the significance of their own comments or what is interesting to the audience. It's their story, and often they are blasé about it. Perhaps they have shared their story so many times that they gloss over parts that need emphasis. I find that, as an interviewer, it is important to stop the interviewee when something significant is said, and say something like, "Sorry, let me interject. You said that you got turned down over 100 times before someone invested?"

One of my favorite interviews I've ever done was the one I conducted with Paul Henderson at an ELO Forum in Toronto. In Canada, for people 55 and over, Paul Henderson is a household name and an iconic figure. It goes all the way back to 1972: the time of the Cold War. The NHL at that time was composed of North American, and primarily Canadian, hockey players. Naturally, NHL players thought they were the best in the world, and the quality of USSR players was unknown.

In 1972, the Canada-USSR Hockey Summit was organized. This would be an 8-game series between Canadian all-stars and a USSR team. Many predicted an 8-0 Canadian sweep over the equivalent of the Washington

Generals, and along with it proof of the superiority of a capitalist system. Unfortunately, the series didn't start well, and it was in danger of finishing badly. Canada needed to win the last game in order to win the series. The game was tied going into the final seconds. Then, miraculously Paul Henderson scored. Canada won the series, by the slightest of margins, and Paul Henderson was a hero. He quickly became a Canadian celebrity.

Years later, I had the chance to get to know Paul Henderson, and then interview him on the podium. I joked with people afterwards that I did a phenomenal job of interviewing Paul. I said, "Hi Paul." He spoke. I said, "Thank you, Paul."

Paul, even into his late 70s and after bouts of cancer, was an energetic and enthusiastic speaker. Magnetism oozed from every pore of his body. He was articulate and passionate. Nobody cared about my own experience, or where I was sitting when Paul Henderson scored. My focus was on getting him to tell his story and have listeners imagine where they were when he scored "The Goal of the Century."

LAW #43: Bring out the best in your interviewee through preparation, active listening, skillful questioning, a non-judgmental attitude, and a humble spirit.

D.44: THE WORKSHOP

A workshop is typically defined as a session on a specific topic, lasting between a half day and a couple of days, and is put on by an outside presenter to a company or group of executives interested in a particular topic. In essence, it is like a short course.

All the basic laws of public speaking apply, but there are some unique dynamics. If you host a workshop, you will be able to establish rapport with the group over an extended period of time—so you want to be building it, not losing it. You don't want people to tune out within the first minutes—it will be hard to get them back, especially when you will be with them over an extended period of time.

Think of the audience as your friends. They are not the enemy. They are not to be insulted or to be belittled. You may be thinking, *what's the point of saying this? This is painfully obvious. Who would get in front of a crowd and then antagonize them?* Well, that happens—more often than one might imagine.

I had one speaker bark out phrases like, "You need to understand this!" and "Read your history books!" Hectoring from the front is typically not a good way to bond with your audience. That speaker could have used a bit more self awareness. Let me tell you that story.

A company I was part of years ago organized some personal development workshops. The events were organized by the HR Department, and everyone in the company was required to attend. The general purpose of the events was to encourage personal development, focus on goals, and develop a positive corporate culture.

There were about 50 of us in the room, at round tables. The instructor had a military background from another country, far, far away. He had a shaved head, had been working his bicep curls incessantly, wore a shirt two buttons too tight for his torso, and spoke like a drill sergeant. He gave the impression from the get-go that he had us for a limited amount of time, and he was going to whip us into his version of intellectual shape. He spoke in a machine-gun, staccato style. His rhetorical questions came across like a battering ram. He had a thick accent, which made it hard to always make out clearly what he was saying. He was fond of bellowing: "You need to hear this." Better yet were the commands, "You need to put away your cellphones," and, "You need to put away your laptops." I guess none of us realized that we had been miraculously transported back to Kindergarten.

We had just gotten started when he belted out, "You, in the back, put away your cellphone." He was talking to my colleague, who needed to be in touch with his office. At that moment, he had been responding to an inquiry. I thought right away that this was a bizarre action for a workshop leader to take. I had never been at a presentation where the speaker was so combative, and he seemed to literally want to get into an argument with participants. My colleague ignored him and muttered some expletives. I was listening, biting my tongue.

Our workshop leader was, however, not done sharing the love. Whenever I am at a presentation, I like to have my laptop open and take notes directly onto my laptop. I find that my handwriting is very slow and laborious (I think it is because I am left-handed). So, I was at the back table, where no one could actually see me, unless they turned around, and I had my laptop on my lap, listening intently and taking notes.

Then, as robo-presenter is going through his presentation he barks out, "put the laptop away! I said *put the laptop away!*" Then he addressed the whole group, as if it were a teachable moment, saying that people who have their laptops open are not paying attention because there are too many distractions on their laptop, and research has proven that people retain more information if they take notes by hand. In fact, I was very focused on taking notes, which for me is far more effective when I can input them into a Word document rather than writing by hand.

As robo-presenter was yelping at me, I simply ignored him. I didn't put away my laptop, and just kept taking notes. The rest of the group was quite passive, simply waiting for him to stop berating audience members and to get on with the substance of his talk.

Within the first few minutes of his all-day session, it became clear that his presentation was something to be endured rather than to be enjoyed.

Since this was a company sanctioned event, and someone from the company had paid good money to have him train the company members, attendees went through the motions. The reality was, however, that due to his demeanor and actions, he was quite unlikable, coming across as insolent and obnoxious.

To avoid this scenario and to succeed as a public speaker, you simply need to follow the laws in this book. The great speakers I have mentioned in this book are masters. They are likable. They are welcoming. They assume the audience is smart—perhaps smarter than they really are. They speak to them as equals, not as if they were superior to their audience. They are never condescending.

There is a big difference between the following two approaches to introducing a theatrical reference. The first option would be to say: "As all of you will recall in Shakespeare's classic play of Romeo and Juliet, the Montagues and Capulets were unexpectedly brought together by the love between their offspring." This introduction makes the reasonable assumption that the listeners know the outline of the story, which is part of the canon of Western literature.

The second option: "Shakespeare was an English playwright who wrote many plays including Romeo and Juliet. If you don't know that, read more! Romeo was from the Montague family. Juliet was from the Capulet family. The two families were brought together by their offspring." You can easily see the difference between these two approaches.

The public speaking rule of success is to connect with the audience. Be likable. Be positive. Thank them for their time and attention. Assume they know items that constitute general knowledge. If they feel positive and uplifted, they will view you as helping them. You always want your audience to feel smarter, not stupider.

LAW #44: Doing a workshop well means connecting with the audience by understanding them, relating to them, and building a relationship with them.

D.45: FOUR WEDDINGS

Weddings are a great occasion to observe public speaking. It's often more fun to go to weddings where you are not connected with the group putting it on, but rather are an outside observer. In homage to the film *Four Weddings and a Funeral*, I have selected four teachable moments in public speaking I have observed at various weddings.

Wedding #1: Do the Toast, Don't Be the Toast

The big day had arrived. To the surprise of everyone who knew him, the groom was getting married. The engagement had lasted about eight months and the planning had been ongoing all the way until big day. There were, of course, many details to wade through, from the photographer and the flowers, to the dinner venue and out of town guests.

Everything was choreographed and planned down to the last minute. After the church service, there would be a break for photographs, and then the attendees would go to a prestigious downtown hotel ballroom. The wedding party would get settled at the head table, and then the evening program would begin. There would be a welcome from the co-emcees, then a toast to the groom, and then a toast to the bride. Finally, the minister would say a short prayer, and everyone would move on to dinner. After a long afternoon of getting married and taking photos, that would be a fun evening.

Everyone had been given guidelines. The toast to the groom would be performed by one of his aunts. The bride chose her dad's best friend to do her toast. They had been each asked to share some brief thoughts about the couple, and to keep it to 3–4 minutes.

Of course, as with any occasion, an outline of the evening was given to the hotel staff and explained to them so they could serve the meals at the correct time. With any event, there is a limit to everyone's patience and endurance, and the plan was to be done by 10 p.m. People had driven in from up to an hour and a half distance, so bad timing would have dissipated good will. The timing was important.

The groom's aunt came to the podium and made her toast. She started with some remarks about her nephew, and tied it together nicely with some general comments. She was very competent and polished, and did a great job. She definitely made the top 10% of speakers.

Then came the fellow chosen to make the toast to the bride. As he came up, he shot an approving look at his buddy, the father of the groom. His opening words struck fear into the heart of the listeners. "Joe and I first got to know one another 42 years ago." It was all downhill from there, and it took almost 40 minutes to get to the bottom of the hill. The hotel staff, standing ready to bring in the food, eventually gave up (or rigor mortis was setting in) and put down the trays and retreated to the kitchen. Not only was the speech long, it was boring and rambling. He went on and on about his friendship with Joe, and all the fine things they did together. It had nothing to do with the bride. It was a stream of conscious reminiscence with no beginning or end. Finally, the speaker ran out of recollections and abruptly declared, "Let's toast to the bride."

That was an enthusiastic toast, as it was confirmation that the rambling speech was over. This speech single-handedly disrupted the entire event. The hot dinner was cold and now almost stale dated, the event finished late, and people began sneaking out early. The people who did hang around towards the end did so out of obligation, not because of joy. That speaker made a massive blunder. He was toast: he didn't give a very good one.

The key to avoiding this mistake is to think about the context. This was not an appropriate opportunity for the person to reminisce about the good old days. The context was that he had been asked to do a toast, and provided with 3–4 minutes. When you give a toast, you are a small part of the bigger event. You need to think about a couple of things about the person you're toasting, say you are happy for them, and declare a toast.

Wedding #2: Lesson From the Priest

Most of us have been to weddings. There is, of course, typically an officiant conducting the wedding and then delivering a message to the happy couple.

This wedding was held in a spectacular Catholic cathedral. Flowers adorned the ends of the pews and the altar piece. There was a singer providing amazing vocals as background music. It was a glorious summer day. Months of preparation and expense had culminated in this moment. The monkey wrench in the piece, as is typically the case, is the human element.

The couple was Catholic by background, but not practicing. Apparently, there was some premarital counselling, but it must have been brief. They appeared to be meeting the priest for the first time at the wedding. It was to be a small, intimate and personal affair. The priest sallied forth to the front of the church and began the remarks as one would have expected. One got the impression that this might have been one of several weddings he was doing on a busy Saturday in a hot summer.

"I'd like to welcome you to the wedding of Samantha and Dirk," he began with due pomp and circumstance. "We are glad you could join us." The maid of honor, who was closest to the priest, was energetically whispering to him and trying to get his attention, to no avail. The priest went on a bit, and then asked Samantha and Dirk to rise and join him at the front. The problem: the couple's names were Sarah and Derrick. All carefully laid plans went out a stain glass window. Rowan Atkinson had arrived.

From that moment on most people, including the couple, were likely wondering how much longer this ceremony would go, and how much more damage there would be before the end. Fortunately, the priest could read from the script the rest of the way. Unwittingly, though, the priest became the center of attention. This scenario violated most of the laws of public speaking. Be prepared. It's not about you—it's about them. You don't want to be remembered for all the wrong reasons.

Wedding #3: Lesson from the Father of the Bride

On the other hand, I have been at countless weddings where the officiant had done an outstanding job, performing with grace and aplomb and then delivering a fine message that was carefully crafted around the couple.

Another aspect of a wedding, however, is the speeches made by various parties. Typically, the parents will offer some remarks to share a bit about their adult child getting married and to welcome the betrothed into their new family. Again, during these speeches, all the laws of public speaking apply. People will give you a pass to some extent, but you still want people to enjoy the wedding. I have seen the entire range of parental performances. Usually the parental remarks are limited to 4–5 minutes for each side, as that allows for up to 4 people to make a remark in 20 minutes. The key is that a wedding has a lot of moving parts, and a few things going over time will disrupt the flow of the entire event.

I have seen many parents get up, make thoughtful, sincere, insightful and humorous remarks. There are other situations, as well. In one case, the father of the bride got up and was already sobbing on his way to the podium. He got to the microphone and broke down even more. He eventually blabbered out some message along the lines of loving his daughter very much. When it came to his new son-in-law, he was not much better. Over the course of five minutes, he said: "I love you, man... man, I love you... love, both of you... I know you'll be a great partner for my daughter... I love you both..." At this point, those assembled were rooting for him simply to finish and sit down before the coffee and desserts ran out.

Especially when it is an emotionally charged event, have some notes with a few bullet points so that you don't forget anything. There is not much excuse for letting your kids down, given that you typically have a lot of preparation time for a wedding.

Wedding #4: Lesson from the Bride

You never know where the fun is going to come from at a wedding. It's like a surprise gift. There are so many moving parts. Of course, one of the highlights is the speeches by the wedded couple. Since they are usually towards the end of the wedding program, they are typically not that long—"typically" being the operative word. I was at one wedding where the bride left no stone unturned in terms of highlighting a panoply of past relationships, encounters, and experiences. It was clearly an exercise in creative imagination and self-aggrandizement.

She started by acknowledging most people she had met, near and far. "I'd like to acknowledge the Japanese friend, Tomoko, who I met on the way to Mt Fuji on one of my previous visits to Japan. We shared a wonderful conversation in the line up to the washroom and in adjoining stalls, and though our time was short and we didn't stay in touch, I wanted to mention that." We knew we were in for a long evening; we didn't know if the open bar could outlast the bride. She then moved on to people she had actually met. "Oh, and my friend, Dan, a great businessperson, a true financial genius, thank you for your wise insights during our two-week relationship and the opportunity to sell soap to family and friends." Apparently, he was on his third multilevel marketing scheme.

Of course, at a wedding the bride and groom have much leeway and the gathered assembly will be magnanimous. At the same time, if you are the bride or groom there is no need to take advantage of people's good will.

Again, all the public speaking laws apply. The longer you go, the more people tune out, so it's counterproductive to take too much time. Keep your remarks short and sweet, even on your wedding day.

LAW #45: A wedding is a great opportunity to contribute positively to the experience of a couple and family—don't make yourself memorable for all the wrong reasons.

D.46: ...AND A FUNERAL

It was a sparse and relatively compact church in which the grieving family gathered that day, white on the outside and spartan, hardwood pews on the inside. In keeping with Mennonite tradition, the walls were unadorned to keep the focus at the front of the room. The day was hot and the fans overhead were working hard, laboring to contribute some comfort to the solemn occasion.

They had gathered for the funeral services of their devout and devoted grandmother, "Oma," who had passed on at the age of 95. She had lived through the Russian Revolution, the First World War, and the Second World War before going on to plant roots in Canada. She led a life well-lived, and she was well loved, with a wonderful story of thanksgiving to tell.

The pastor in charge of the proceedings came up to make his remarks. Although he didn't know Oma well, he looked a tad emotional. He began his message. "She was a fine lady. She reminds me of my own recently-departed mother. She was lovely. She will be dearly missed. She had an impact on her family. She was a woman of virtue." This was a heartfelt tribute.

There was a problem, however. He was not talking about the woman, Oma, that all of them had come to honor. Soon after saying that the dearly beloved were there to honor their mother and grandmother, the minister said that their grandmother reminded him of his own mother. This then led him on a sidebar that consumed most of his message, until they were all listening to someone praise his own mother at the funeral of their grandmother.

It should have been an abomination to the Lord. People kept hoping it would stop, and that he would get back on the rails. He never did. He just kept digging a bigger hole. When he finally finished, there were a number of very emphatic, silent "amens," which, if not for the gravity of the occasion that prevented them from being uttered, would have blown the roof off the place.

Now, that funeral is remembered for all the wrong reasons, though the pastor surely had not intended this result. It was likely one of the most misguided messages that any of the family and friends had ever heard. It didn't make him very popular at the meal in the church basement afterwards. Worse, it undermined his credibility and professionalism.

There are a number of important lessons here. You may be called up to speak at a funeral, and you may have known the person well (friend or close family member) or not (an extended family member stepping in to help). Either way, remember why you are there and what you are trying to do: you are at a funeral to honor the deceased person, and to comfort the family. It is a solemn occasion calling for a deft touch. It's not about you.

You should be prepared. Ask the family what they appreciated about the departed family member. Focus on what you knew about the deceased. Extemporaneous speaking can be a disaster.

LAW #46: If you have the opportunity to speak at a funeral, remember the basic rules of public speaking. Focus on the purpose, the context, and the time constraints, and be a comfort to people in their time of need.

D.47: UNIVERSITY LECTURING

I decided to include a chapter on university lecturing for two reasons: first, I and many readers have sat through umpteen university lectures, and have views on how they could have been better. Second, you may be asked to do a guest presentation at a university, and thus it is good to understand the dynamics of that educational context.

University lecturing is a form of public speaking, in the sense that there is a person at the front of the room flapping her gums, and there are a number of people who are trying to listen and learn. The difference, however, is that the instructor is teaching a certain subject matter over a series of sessions. There is a lot of content, the students have their textbooks, and they are expected to do a lot of additional reading and work. And something being uttered may end up on an exam.

University lecturing is a different form of public speaking, where many of the basic rules don't apply. The nature of the academic world is that professors at large academic institutions are expected to do research, publish their work, and bring recognition to their university. Excellence in teaching is generally not ranked highly in terms of their contribution to their institution. In fact, the reward for doing a great overall job is to be given fewer classes to teach.

This varies between institutions. Typically, the larger and more prestigious institutions are research focused and expect little on the teaching front. A smaller university is often more student-focused; it needs the enrollment, and therefore caters to students. In that environment, the professors receive training on teaching and communication techniques.

I taught at a university school of business for ten years. I taught business law, entrepreneurship, strategic planning, international business, entrepreneurial finance and leadership. I have also sat through lectures at four universities, in Canada, the US and the UK. I have guest lectured at universities around the world, and I lead and teach in the Entrepreneurial Leaders Programme at Wycliffe Hall, University of Oxford.

My own experiences varied. In my undergraduate years, especially the first two years, the teaching was generally abysmal. This is a common scenario with large introductory classes of up to 300 students in the arts, psychology and English. The professor is a tiny figure at the front of the classroom going through the motions of covering material, not caring whether it was interesting or not.

I still remember one class vividly. The entrance doors to the auditorium were at the back of the room, with tiered seating down to the front, where there was a lectern and an overhead projector. There was a side entrance which led directly to the podium. We students would shuffle into the auditorium from the back of the room and get ready for class, and at around the appointed time, the professor would enter the classroom from the side entrance and start talking in a monotone voice. He would simply proceed through the material, with the sole objective of completing the task, rather than teaching anything. He was a bit of an introvert by all appearances and seemed to simply be content talking to himself on stage with an audience watching him.

He didn't ask if there were any questions. With so many students that was neither possible nor desirable. His job was to "teach"—get up and start talking and get through the material. At the end of 55 minutes it was mission accomplished. At the same time, very little if anything was communicated or taught. Further, virtually every law of public speaking was violated in the process.

There was no incentive for the professor to do a better job. It was irrelevant to his job security. He had tenure, after all. Of course, this was confusing for first- and second-year students who were at the university to, well, be taught. We soon realized that there was a fundamental difference in objectives and that there would need to be a lot of self-learning. Did it have to be that way? Is it always that way?

Of course, it is impossible to generalize among all universities everywhere and I can only speak to my experiences, which, however, have been relatively varied and extensive. Going from my undergraduate degree, where I focused on history and economics, to law school, was a jarring shift. Everything that I was missing in my undergrad, I received at law school. I went from a large state school to McGill Law School, where the teaching was generally excellent, and one class in particular was outstanding.

A first-year course for all students was basic contract law. In my case, it was taught by Professor G. Blaine Baker. He was a master of the Socratic dialogue, which is a well-known technique used in law school classrooms to engage the class by asking questions and calling on students. Professor Baker made it a priority to get to know students' names, their backgrounds, and likely their capabilities, as well.

He would begin a class, introduce the topic briefly and then start asking questions. "What are the basic facts of Smith v. Jones? What was the main issue? Do you agree? What were the main legal principles? What precedents were relied on? What was the majority opinion? Do you agree with the minority in dissent?"

What made the classes so interesting was that Professor Baker would engage a wide range of students. He would call them by name. He would ask for their view. He would summarize it, confirm it was correct, and then ask another student for the opposing view. He would then summarize that, and call on another student. He would wield his intellect like a fencing sword, rather than the big sword of William Wallace. As the discussion become more detailed and intricate, he would call on others.

He would say, "Dr. Horwood, do you agree with the forgoing analysis by Mr. Jones?" I remember turning around in my front seat and thinking, "Who is Dr. Horwood?" Yes, indeed, there was a fellow in our class with a PhD. Professor Baker liked a bit of decorum, and I think a subtle way to raise the intellectual bar, and refer to "Bob" as Dr. Horwood.

The classes led by Professor Baker were riveting, engaging, and seemed to fly by. It was like being in the presence of an intellectual conductor in full control of the class, the subject matter and the students. He knew many of the students and clearly cared. Decades later, I remember these first-year classes vividly. Professor Baker was a well-deserved multiple-time winner of the best teaching award.

On the other hand, what if you are asked to give a guest presentation at a university? How should you approach it? Here are several pointers.

The basic laws of public speaking apply, with some nuances. First is the context. What is the class, and what is the purpose? I brought in guest presenters regularly to my entrepreneurship classes. This worked out well. The students liked to hear about an individual's business journey.

The level of engagement by students may vary. You may come in excited to share your insights, and yet the class may seem uninterested and unresponsive. Why? Students are practical. Even at the university level, students will think: "Is this going to be on the exam?" Don't be discouraged if the level of engagement is low. Just come in, as always, with the idea that if you can positively impact even one person, then it is all worthwhile.

Part of the context is that students are used to getting lot of content and an outline and notes. Using a slideshow would be quite acceptable, and leaving a copy of it for students is a good idea. University classes generally go at a certain pace, since they are spread over a four-month period. There is typically no need to cram everything into a single class: there is always next time.

As a guest in someone else's class, this poses a challenge, as the class is acclimatized to a certain approach, pace, and style. Many times, a guest lecturer is a jarring shift in direction. A good approach is often to insist on using a Q&A format. Thus, the instructor can set the usual tone, and you can fit into that.

Another rule is that a university class is not an opportunity for pontificating. I had one business contact come in as a guest lecturer to share his story. This was the first time he had been invited to a university to do a guest lecture. While he shared his story, he also viewed it as a once-in-a-lifetime opportunity to share his views on the meaning of life and many other things unrelated to his business.

For businesspeople, doing a guest lecture for a bunch of undergraduates may not be that appealing, other than something to add to the CV beyond simply community service. Undergrads are in the business of acquiring knowledge. They will ask some questions, but they are more on the receiving end.

By contrast, being part of an MBA class is different. MBA students want to demonstrate what they know, so you are there to give them an opportunity to speak. A little knowledge can be a dangerous thing. In that context, it's best to be prepared for many questions, and to give the class plenty of time to speak.

Executive education is a different level of university lecturing. A good example is the annual Entrepreneurial Leaders Programme that I teach each summer at Wycliffe Hall, University of Oxford. The cohort of approximately 25 participants is composed of highly experienced business leaders. This program is taught over a one-week period in August. We have a core team of lecturers, as well as guest lecturers we bring in. One of the biggest lessons I have learned is the humility and understated confidence of truly successful people. I recall that we were discussing some corporate governance related issues. I was thinking, "What am I doing talking about this topic to these people? I'm not sure I'm going to add much!" I made a few comments, and then asked for people to share some of their experiences.

Nothing. Silence. Then it struck me: no one had anything to prove. No one felt the need to demonstrate how smart they were, how big their company was, or how many boards they were on. Slowly, one person said, "Well, perhaps, I can add a point here," and eventually we got on a bit of a roll. There was a great discussion, with tremendous insights, but most importantly, all these leaders had a high degree of emotional intelligence: one of the key aspects of life and business success.

LAW #47: Lecturing at a university is a unique public speaking opportunity. Different classes and contexts will require customized approaches.

D.48: THE PERILS OF PANELS

I knew within minutes that the panel would not end well. I was invited to be part of a discussion at a business conference in Singapore. I was one of five panelists for a 45-minute session. We were each supposed to have 5 minutes to say our piece, and then we were going to have a group discussion. The inexperienced panel chair launched into the panel by explaining his own background and then giving some context—in fact, a lot of context. I remember thinking that this was a lot of talking.

After the moderator finished his introduction, the first panelist started to speak. That ate up 15 minutes. It didn't take much mathematical skill to figure out that, at the rate we were going, it was going to be tight for time. The moderator then went through the rest of the panelists, with each one taking a bit too much time, and by the time he got to me, we were close to out of time. I had one minute to deliver a five-minute overview. It was quite maddening, after preparing remarks and looked forward to a discussion, to have it scuttled by ineptitude. When you are invited onto a panel, ask a lot of questions about the how it will be moderated, the order of presenters, and what the format will be for asking questions.

The same dynamics apply if you are organizing a panel. You need to take an active role as the host, controlling the microphone and treating it as a Q&A. If not, you will experience the perils of panels. One time, I organized a panel with three speakers. It was to be a total of 20 minutes, with each presenter having 5 minutes to say their piece, and then I allocated 5 minutes to myself for a wrap up. The first panelist went 15 minutes, the next went 10 minutes and the last one went exactly 5 minutes. All three of them were businesspeople and not professional speakers. Once they got rolling, it was impossible to control them. I was standing at the podium and the three panelists were seating at a rectangular table at the other side of the platform. They had their own microphones. This was a mistake. I no longer host panels unless I am controlling the microphone and using a Q&A format.

We have discussed the digital environment in Section C. In the realm of panels, a digital environment offers some advantages. Panel discussions are much easier to control in terms of interjecting comments and, if necessary, as a last resort, muting someone. I have found that in an online format that panelists are more amenable to the direction of the host.

A panel is no better than the moderator, who is responsible for setting and monitoring parameters. When not done well, all panelists will be equally unhappy, along with yourself.

LAW #48: The perils of panels are plenty; do your best within the provided parameters to be professional, succinct, and gracious.

D.49 SERMONIZING

I am not sure how many readers of this book will be doing a sermon, but I include this brief chapter because sermons and those who deliver them provide many great lessons related to public speaking. I have probably listened live to over 2,000 sermons in my lifetime (I point that out to show experience rather than to claim that I have improved proportionately). In addition, I have, like many people, have watched great preachers, via TV and now on YouTube. I have delivered sermons in various churches over the years. Likely my first true speaking opportunity was delivering a sermon at my home church when I was 21. I have read various books on preaching. Delivering a sermon has some unique characteristics, but at the same time, many of the same dynamics as general speaking engagements still apply. Many of the best speakers now and in history were pastors—one of the most notable, of course, was the Rev. Martin Luther King. Jr. There is Billy Graham who preached to tens of millions around the globe. He was sometimes accused of having a simple message, which was true; but people understood the message. It resonated with them.

Sermons are unique for several reasons. First, and most importantly, is that the personal character and credibility of the deliverer is more important than with other forms of public speaking. A person could be an expert in a particular subject, like pandemic control, and yet their private moral behaviour would largely be irrelevant. When you hear a speaker at a conference on, say, the best practices of beekeeping, you wouldn't wonder about their personal life. With a sermonizer, however, most of their messages would have a moral component directed at changing the listener's behavior. A natural response, in addition to looking in the mirror, is to wonder about the sermonizer, "Are they walking the talk?" If the sermon were about, for instance, avoiding gossip, and you knew the sermonizer was a gossiper, or engaged in morally questionable behaviour generally, then you would likely discount everything they had to say—even though they could make good points about why not to gossip.

Second, the listeners are generally familiar with the source material (the Bible). This is unique because, in other public speaking contexts, the listeners may be more of a blank slate: you can assume that they have little background knowledge for your speech. If you are speaking about pandemics and how they spread, there are likely few people in an audience who would have more knowledge about the topic. By contrast, when you are doing a sermon, this is generally not the case. If you are speaking about the parable of the Good Samaritan, most people know the ending.

Third, people listening to a sermon often leave room for a supernatural, "God-moment" type of experience. They are not just listening; they want God to touch them and speak to them in a profound way. They are looking to the pastor to be a channel, and to deliver a divine message to the listener. To some extent, therefore, the qualities of a sermonizer as a public speaker can be eclipsed by an individual's receptivity to a particular message at that point in time.

Fourth, sermons are unique in terms of the listeners' specific expectations regarding the length and style of the sermon. Typically, there will be an introduction identifying or reading the passage being discussed, some background explanation, some stories, three insights and then a conclusion. The parishioner may have heard hundreds of sermons and may have listed to the particular pastor many times. They have expectation, before the sermon begins, as to how things will play out.

In light of these points, if you are ever asked to deliver a sermon, here is a start on how to deliver a good one. The basic laws apply, but there are some nuances. Many sermons are 20-30 minutes long and have around three points, often a mnemonic of something like "S-I-N" or the "three P's." Here is the basic way to assess a good sermon: use the one-minute test (see Law #3).

An effective sermon must have a very clear structure and format. For starters, think very, very carefully about the title. Have a title that is clear, proactive and assertive. A poor title is something like, "What Should We Build On?" Instead, try something more assertive and definitive like, "Build on Rock, Not Sand." The title should then be repeated occasionally throughout the sermon as the core theme. The speaker should then build a set of points (the mind can remember three points) around that theme, with every story and example tied back into that titular theme. The three points should be easy to remember.

Poor sermons often have the feel of a random series of points strung together with no cohesive theme. They go on and on, and then eventually stop. By contrast, in a good message there is momentum through a well-structured presentation and towards the final goal. People can understand the message and get comfortable with it.

I remember a pastor from almost 15 years ago. He had a clear message. I recall that he had a string of great stories, excellent quotes, insightful personal observations, and a soothing voice with an expressive delivery. He wasted no words. I also remember another pastor equally vividly. He spoke far too fast. He threw in cynical comments, which looks and sounds bad. Cynicism is amplified from a podium. He sped over points that required explanation because he had so much ground to cover. He threw in too many big words that seemed to reflect a desire to be learned rather than clear. At one point, he even shouted out "YOO-HOO!!!" for dramatic effect. It came across as odd, not effective. He was also trying to cover too much territory for the time provided.

How does one provide a great sermon, especially when you are a guest presenter? While this book provides the 50 laws, here are a few points worth highlighting. First, work to establish connection with people. Don't set yourself against them. Second, start off slowly and allow people to get comfortable with you at the podium. Third, make good use of dead space. Knowing when to pause and let your words sink in is very powerful. Fourth, avoid providing too much detail, or the audience will not remember the main point of the message. Finally, always maintain structure and focus.

LAW #49: Giving a sermon is a unique speaking opportunity to have an impact on people; remember the unique aspects of a sermon which make it unlike most other public speaking scenarios.

D.50: YOUR HONOR

Have you been fortunate enough to have been honored in some way? When you have been chosen to receive an award, you are often then expected to deliver an acceptance speech. This is a high honor. In some cases, you will have time to prepare, as you will have been notified in advance. In other cases, the recognition may be a surprise. Another, perhaps more common, honor for people is when they are reaching certain life milestones, such as wedding anniversaries, birthday celebrations, or retirement parties. In all of these cases, the honoree typically makes some remarks.

Of course, all the laws in this book apply, but there are some specific dynamics involved in an acceptance speech that are worth noting. First, let's look at the scenario of accepting an award—perhaps not an Academy Award, but an award nonetheless. What do people generally think of the Academy Awards? People watch for the awards themselves, and not the acceptance speeches. The acceptance speeches are almost unbearable—the ratings have been plummeting for several years, now reaching record lows. You can, however, use your Public Speaking Laws of Success Scorecard® (found at the end of this book) and learn from the acceptance speeches. It is sometimes shocking to see actors, who we have only seen in situations where every word and gesture predetermined, suddenly left to speak their own words. An Oscar acceptance speech often show how good writers are.

Academy Award acceptance speeches generally reflect all the bad principles of public speaking. First, recipients tend to forget that they are not bigger than the event. The Academy Awards Ceremony already runs far too long and is too boring, even while trying to limit the number and length of acceptance speeches. A recipient going beyond their allotted time is self-centered. This begs the question: where's the remote control? Remember, it's not about you and that you are not bigger than the event.

Second, one should be concise. It is downright comical when speakers blabber on about everyone they need to thank, until they get down to third cousins, fourth wives and their two dogs. Why bother rattling off the names of a bunch of people and pets? The audience will not process their names, and, if they do, they will soon be forgotten. If you try to cram too much in, you will end up speaking faster, which means even less will be absorbed. You'll be like an Oscar recipient racing to beat the time limit, to outlast the exit music.

Third, this is not the time to pontificate. Don't say things like, "It's about time I got the award—people like me should have been honored long ago!" Don't use the opportunity to bite than hand that feeds you. Similarly, don't think to yourself, "Now that I have the platform, I want to talk about my pet passion, because everyone needs to listen to me." Focus on the award you are receiving.

Fourth, most Oscar winners don't emit class. "This is my moment of glory and I'm going to milk it for all it's worth," is more their mentality. Thankfully, there are exceptions. Every once in a while an actor will speak articulately and intelligently, make some good remarks, speak with pace, and finish on time. A British accent seems to help. The audience thinks, "Wow, that's an intelligent and articulate person. This is a sight to behold." Whenever you are recognized in any matter, be gracious.

So, the Academy Awards are relevant to you as a learning experience. When you receive an award, you need to remember that you are not bigger than the event. Honor the show organizers. Stay on time. Remember why you are there. Next time you receive an award, from the Academy or otherwise, bear those lessons in mind.

What about the other situations where you are being honored: your 25th wedding anniversary, perhaps, or your retirement party after 30 years, or your 65th birthday? People are there to see you and, yes, to hear from you. Don't let them down. Try to think through your remarks and have a bit of structure. Be thoughtful, kind and considerate. Conjure up memories in your speech that others can relate to. Tell stories about situations that are meaningful to you. I have heard many excellent heartfelt speeches by people from all walks of life and they can have a significant emotional impact. While the event is about you, at least to some extent, be mindful that it is much better to focus on all the people who have added to your enjoyment in life.

> **LAW #50:** If you have the privilege of being honored in some way, then confirm that the organizers made the right choice by accepting the honor in a dignified and gracious manner.

CONCLUSION

I mentioned this at the start of the book, but it bears repeating: learning to speak in public is a bit like learning a language. If you are too embarrassed to try speaking a new language because you are not entirely fluent, you will have a hard time learning anything. If, on the other hand, you dive in and start speaking, with an intention to learn, you will improve significantly. It is the same with public speaking. You need to get started in order to learn. Yes, you need guidance through the fundamentals of public speaking so that you are able to work on the basics, but the true key is that you need to start practicing—right now.

You only learn by doing—not by waiting to be perfect. You can be better than 90% of all public speakers by following and applying the laws of success in this book—guaranteed. How can I make such a claim? Experience. I have seen these laws in action many times over. The most basic laws for public speaking success are continually violated. I believe this is the case because people are asked to speak in public, not because they are skilled at doing so, but rather because of their expertise, availability, connections, or a particular role in an organization.

This book, though, will get you in the top of the field. You need to develop your craft over time and look for many opportunities to practice. Many of the best speakers have spent a lifetime developing their expertise.

In addition to this process there is one other core principle that will ultimately determine your effectiveness as a public speaker. You must strike the appropriate balance of (1) what you say and (2) how you say it. It sounds simple, and yet it's hard to execute. If you can combine both, you will be among the top of all public speakers.

Much of that outcome lies beyond the scope of this book. Let me explain. This book has focused on the public speaking laws of success: the mechanics; key principles; the digital environment; and applications. Let's say you master the 50 public speaking laws of success. 50% of your success is still dependent upon an element that I haven't covered: the content! If you have nothing to say, it won't matter how well you say it.

To succeed as a speaker, you need to be knowledgeable in your field. You need to be an expert, an established authority, or an author/researcher. A great example is Larry C. Farrell, to whom I referred earlier in this book. Larry (and his publishers) can confidently claim that he is "the world's most experienced authority on researching and teaching entrepreneurship." He has used his programs to teach over 6 million people, in 9 languages, over 40 years. He is a rare combination of being both an expert on content and being a great public speaker. Alternatively, a great speaker may not be an expert, but instead have particular life experiences that people want to hear about. Say you rowed your dinghy across the Atlantic for 90 days, ate sharks for breakfast, fought off pirates, and lived to tell tall tales. What was it really like? Pray tell. The key point is that you need to master your content, or there will be a lid on your impact.

The other part of the equation is how you communicate your content. Effective public speakers can influence thousands of people simply through the way they deliver their thoughts. Of course, there many famous examples, from Winston Churchill to the Rev. Martin Luther King, Jr. Decades later, hearing "we shall never surrender…" and "I have a dream…" still sends shivers up one's spine. Shakespeare, over 400 years earlier, has his well-crafted lines etched in rhetorical infinity through characters such as Hamlet ("to be or not to be…"). Well-crafted and skillfully-delivered thoughts can have great impact. While most of us likely will not have the same impact as these historical giants, we can still influence many people and make a difference in their individual lives.

A number of speakers have told me over the years that their motivation is to impact at least one person in the audience through their presentations. We have likely all been in an audience where a particular speaker resonated with us—maybe with others, too, but particularly with us. To some extent, public speaking is a sacred opportunity to impact others positively. You may motivate listeners, or get them to correct a particular course of action, and you will have a better chance for greater impact if you can communicate your message effectively.

To sum up this book, I hope that the 50 public speaking laws of success will help you to be a great presenter, and that it will equip you to more effectively deliver your content and expand your influence. I hope that you will always bring your "A Game" and do your best.

You can decide to improve—and to start now.

PUBLIC SPEAKING LAWS OF SUCCESS SCORECARD®

All of the items below are graded on a scale of 1 (very poor)–10 (excellent):

#	Guidelines / Items	Comments	Score
1	Proper use of time (Start:____ Finish: ____)		
2	Extemporaneous (reference to, not reliance on, notes)		
3	Good start (clear opening line)		
4	Good finish (succinct summary, ending on a strong note)		
5	Good structure: a clear thesis/purpose; balanced and organized remarks in support; and clear progression		
6	Voice control (tone, inflection, tempo)		
7	Appropriate demeanor (suited to the nature of the presentation and the occasion; this varies according to the context, i.e., business, personal, etc.)		

8	Appropriate use of hand gestures, head rotation & eye contact		
9	Clear and articulate pronunciation (i.e., avoiding "gonna", "coulda," "I would like "tuhh," etc.)		
10	Avoidance of "filler" words (i.e., "uhh," "uhm," "like," "you know," etc.) Word # Count _____ _____ _____ _____ _____ _____ _____ _____		
	TOTAL (OUT OF 100)		

ABOUT THE AUTHOR

Richard (Rick) J. Goossen, PhD, is passionate about public speaking. He has been a lifelong student of the craft. He is unique in that he has seen every aspect of being a speaker, from every dimension and in every context. He has given investment presentations, delivered keynotes, spoken at universities, spoken at funerals and weddings, provided sermons, been a university lecturer, done interviews, and given acceptance speeches. He has also taught public speaking, having assisted over 1,000 students with presentation skills. He has organized over 60 business conferences around the world and worked with over 200 of the world's leading speakers. He has analyzed thousands of presentations in every corner of the world.

Rick works at Nicola Wealth (www.NicolaWealth.com), Canada's fastest-growing independent wealth management firm. He is Founder and Chair of Entrepreneurial Leaders Organization ("ELO") (www.ELONetwork.org). He is also the founder and director of the Entrepreneurial Leaders Institute at Wycliffe Hall, University of Oxford where he teaches an annual executive education course titled the "Entrepreneurial Leadership Programme" (www.ELOOxford.com). He continues to speak regularly, both as part of and in addition to his various professional commitments.

Rick has extensive experience doing business in Asia and previously worked in Hong Kong for five years. He has taught entrepreneurship, entrepreneurial finance, strategic management, business law, international business and ethics as an adjunct professor (BBA and MBA programs) and guest lecturer at universities around the world. Rick has edited five books and authored six books related to entrepreneurship. Two of the books he authored are available in six translations.

In terms of credentials, Rick earned a Ph.D. from Middlesex University, London, UK; a Masters of Law (LL.M.) from Columbia University, New York City; a Bachelor of Laws (LL.B.) from McGill University, Montreal; and a Bachelor of Arts (B.A.) (Hons.) (First Class) from Simon Fraser University, Vancouver. Rick was also admitted as Barrister and Solicitor of the Province of British Columbia, Canada and voluntarily withdrew his membership to focus entirely on business pursuits.

THE EXTRAS & A CALL TO ACTION

For Everyone and Every Occasion

If you enjoyed and learned from this book, why not share its insights with your team and company? Rick Goossen teaches the "Public Speaking Laws of Success" online and in person in several formats: keynote, 2 hour and half-day sessions. These training sessions are entertaining, story based and insightful—a winning combination.

The book is used as the foundation of the teaching sessions. In addition, there are many value-added extras not included in this book:
- The Cornerstone of Public Speaking Matrix
- The Pyramid of Public Speaking
- The Public Speaking Quadrants
- 15 Public Speaking Maxims
- 15 Questions for Event Organizers
- Strategic Planning for Public Speakers

Virtually any business can benefit from a company-wide session, especially if public speaking is a common necessity, as it is in professional firms, sales firms, financial institutions and the like.

If you learn and apply the public speaking laws of success, you and your team members will be better than 90% of all other public speakers.

For CEOs

Rick Goossen offers a one-day extensive public speaking coaching session for company founders and owners, CEOs and senior business leaders. This session provides a multiple return on investment. The manner in which top leaders speak in public will add or subtract massive value from their organizations.

Next Steps

For further information go to www.publicspeakinglaws.com.

CPSIA information can be obtained
at www.ICGtesting.com
Printed in the USA
JSHW032352270821
18267JS00002B/112